THE CASE AGAINST SUICIDE

William V. Rauscher

THE CASE
AGAINST
SUICIDE

ST. MARTIN'S PRESS
New York

Library of Congress Cataloging in Publication Data

Rauscher, William V.
  The case against suicide.

  1. Suicide. 2. Suicide-- Moral and religious
aspects. I. Title.
HV6545.R19   179.7   81-5821
ISBN 0-312-12330-2   AACR2

Design by Ed Kaplin

10 9 8 7 6 5 4 3 2 1

First Edition

To
Walter B. Gibson
and
Litzka R. Gibson,
who radiate the energy of life

Contents

Preface

The subject of suicide has intrigued the minds of men and women of all classes and conditions of life. It has intrigued people of all ages, of all societies, and of all degrees of religion and nonreligion. Suicide seems especially interesting to people in times of difficulty and uncertainty. Self-destruction is always a tantalizing way out of the ultimate problems of life. The door of death seems so easy to open. And it is always there in front of us. There is something about death that calls us from the innermost parts of our life.

In our day more and more people, young and old, are not willing to wait for natural death, and so they consider the possibility of circumventing destiny by their own hands. This is not new, of course. Throughout all history, man has sought to rationalize his eternal being. The tantalizing question has always been asked: Is it better to live or to die? And always the answer to that question, whether affirmative or negative, has profoundly affected families, friends, and society as a whole.

It has not been my aim in this book to add to the statistical evidence of the nature and scope of the problem of suicide. There are no charts or graphs or tables here (although the Bibliography will point the interested reader toward such studies). I have recognized at the outset that the threat of suicide lurks in the shadows of every life. I urge my reader to understand at the beginning that education, position, wealth, or poverty does not prevent, nor does it often help, the private life of the person who is thinking about removing himself from this world.

When we take the energy of life into our own hands, thinking to destroy it, we have embarked upon a path of self-deception. It may appear that our action is rational. But are we truly rational unless the ancient and traditional concepts of God the Father are part of our consciousness? True, in moments of deep depression and dark despair, a consciousness of God has not seemed to matter for many people. We do indeed have the capacity to shake our fists at God, to curse his name and ignore his will. But the whole history of the Judeo-Christian religion shows us that such rejection opens the way to wrong decisions. Intellectual, rational decisions without the spiritual component can very well lead to the tragedy of suicide.

When a self-centered individual turns against himself or herself and looks only inward, anything can happen. Suicide is, by definition, a self-centered act. Religion, and more particularly the Judeo-Christian faith, has always opposed self-centeredness. I realize, of course, that religion is not the only way to think about the subject of suicide. That is why I have been careful to review other ways of thinking about it. Nevertheless, my own personal way of thinking and, indeed, my twenty-three years experience as a parish priest dealing with people at the crisis points of their lives, are based on the religious approach to life. It is that basic insight that I wish to offer my readers here.

The reader's personal religious background, how he or she feels about God, will have a great deal to do with whether or not this book is useful. I would like to suggest that the reader bring to this book a positive attitude toward the transcendental dimension of life. For my part, I am convinced that there is consciousness at work in human life that is over and above mere bodily functions.

I earnestly hope that no reader of this book, nor anyone else, for that matter, will commit suicide. But that may be mere fancy. I know very well that someone is taking his or her own life at this very minute! So a major part of my hope is that this book will be a means of insight into another dimension of reality—a dimension that is so often rejected (or entirely unknown) by a person distraught enough to consider taking his or her own life. Reading this book will not make anyone believe in God, but it may open someone's mind to a consideration of what might happen *if* suicide is carried out. Such a person might even be brought to consider the effect of his or her suicide on those who remain.

Many of the people whose stories I have gathered in my research for this book, including those who have come to me for counsel, were not at all the kind one might expect to kill themselves. A surprising number were highly intelligent, well educated, and held positions of great importance. Others were drug-induced suicides, mostly young people. Still others were alcoholics and people who in some unconscious way set out to bring death to themselves; these were the ones who died slowly, day by day.

We tend to think of suicide as a contemporary problem. So it is. But, as I have indicated above, it is also an age-old problem. John Donne, once the eminent intellectual dean of St. Paul's Cathedral, London, admitted that he had contemplated suicide. The famous philosopher and psychologist William James, in a chronic state of depression, pondered his self-destructive impulse. He finally came to the conclusion that life was worth living. He said that one should believe that life is worth living and his belief will help create the fact. Good advice. I myself, in the midst of tensions and almost insurmountable moments of acute loneliness, have pondered the question "Is it worth it?" This book will, I hope, answer that question in the affirmative.

THE CASE AGAINST SUICIDE

Chapter 1

The Case for Suicide?

"Liberty is nothing but the taking of death into our lives. By anticipating death, we are delivered from evil."

—Eugen Rosenstock-Huessy

As I have indicated earlier, we are hearing more frequently these days from those writers and commentators who believe in what they call "rational suicide." And I am quite sure that the public discussion of this idea will be with us for some time to come. It is, therefore, necessary for us to look at this view of suicide.

I want to be clearly understood as being firmly opposed to any notion that there can be such a thing as rational suicide. I think that my reasons for this opposition will become clear in the chapters that follow. Because the subject is being so well-publicized across the country today—on television, in books, and in newspapers, in church seminar groups and in college classrooms—I must

3

present what I hope will be an unbiased and objective account of the case for suicide. The reader deserves to have both sides of the matter available to him or her for serious consideration. All I ask is that the following review of the pro-suicide position not be taken to represent what I myself believe and counsel. I write *as if* the view were my own. *It is not.*

A short essay in a recent issue of *Monday Morning,* the magazine published for United Presbyterian pastors, begins with this paragraph:

"Why can't you let me die?" Doctors and nurses who take care of elderly patients must hear this question or its equivalent over and over again. They ignore it as long as they can, but when pressed for an answer, they explain that their Hippocratic Oath binds them to save human life at all costs. They do not admit, even to themselves, how much of these costs find their way into their own wallets. It does little good for the patient to sign a paper asking that no "heroic procedures" be used to keep him or her alive. They just assume that everyone fears death, and wants to postpone it as long as possible, so anyone who would sign such a request must be out of his or her mind. We are condemned to live on and on, whether we want to or not.[1]

This, in its simplest form, is the basis for the cry for rational suicide. I was interested in seeing how the writer of the article signed it. When I got to the end of the page, I was somewhat startled to see: "Hopeless Case (Pseudonym), Honorably Retired."

And this honorably retired servant of God had entitled his article "Condemned To Live."

In a paragraph following the one I have just quoted, this pastor describes the condition of a great many people today whose lives are being extended by the so-called miracles of modern science. He says:

It looks different to the old, whose bodies are deteriorating. When your joints scream with the pain of arthritis, or your activities are curtailed after a heart attack, or you have to suffer constantly from cancer, any escape looks good, even death. This is especially true for Christians, who confidently expect to spend eternity in heaven's bliss.

So eyesight that fails beyond the power of lenses or surgery to restore it, or hearing so poor no hearing aid can bring one back into the conversation, or memory that becomes such a sieve you can't even remember what you were going to say before you finish the sentence, or senility that keeps you from recognizing your own husband or wife—all prevent life from having any real meaning.

And if you've been independent, even moderately successful, and then find yourself a burden and a care to your loved one, or having to accept government handouts like Social Security, Medicare, or welfare payments in order to survive, when you realize how much the younger taxpayers resent the increasing tax bite—your sense of helplessness and shame become overwhelming.

There ought to be some way that we who no longer are of any use to anybody, even ourselves, could be released from this existence.[2]

The article concludes with a brief prayer: "Help me to endure to the end, since you have condemned me to live."

Anyone who has a loved one in a nursing home or "convalescent" home (nobody ever "convalesces" from old age!) or who tries to minister to such people knows what this man is saying and feeling. To such people the idea of rational suicide is becoming more attractive.

As long ago as 1919, a German psychiatrist named Alfred Hoche used the term "Bilanz-Selbstmord" (balance-sheet suicide), which he recognized as a factor in those suicides that seemed to him to be the result of a logical decision. That is, in his view, a perfectly sane person, under no compulsions except those self-imposed by his or her own notions of religion, morals, law, and an obligation to society, would draw up a balance sheet. Such a sheet would list all of the intolerable, unacceptable aspects of life in one column. In the other column would be listed the chances for an improvement of conditions. If he or she found the sheet to be weighted in favor of death, he or she would deliberately choose that option.

Such a balance-sheet suicide implies, indeed, requires, that a person of mature age be the one involved. Younger people cannot be expected to draw up such a balance sheet. They are still in a position where the conditions of life change radically, almost from day to day. But the older person does not find himself or herself in a position where such reversals for the better are really an option. Vision does *not* recover its clarity; hearing does *not* improve; memory does *not* get better. Friends and relatives who have gone on before do *not* return.

In her book, *Common-Sense Suicide,* Doris Portwood recounts the story of an elderly writer and editor, now long retired, "who built up her suicide over a number of years and left a letter for her friends to describe the process of her thinking and the criteria she used in judging the proper time." In the letter, she said:

> I want to go while I can still enjoy my friends who are so good to me and who I know can still enjoy me, while I can still feel a not too unfavorable balance between happiness and competence and interest and even limited usefulness of my days—and the difficulties and discomforts and pain and expense involved in trying first to maintain that balance and then later merely to prolong life.[3]

I have a friend whose brother is president of a church-sponsored retirement home, which also has a nursing care facility. He tells me that the biggest worry of most elderly people is their health. Next comes their financial situation; after that, or concurrently with it, come family and friends. Often their balance sheet adds up to what has been called a "frying pan or fire" choice: They have no family situation into which they can fit. So whatever security they can find must be bought at the expense of all their property, their Social Security rights, and pension payments. Often such a person is reduced to a helpless, comatose, suffering, long-living condition—living death. And it is a death that costs hundreds of thousands of dollars. Either the family pays for it or, eventually, society in the form of its taxpayers and wage-earners pays for it. (The argument goes on from here: How much longer will the taxpayers be willing to shoulder an annual cost of over $250 billion?)

One estimate indicates that there will be over thirty million people over the age of sixty-five in the United States by the year 2000. And this fact, itself, is raising the rational suicide question not only in America, but especially in Britain where membership in the Euthanasia Society has dramatically soared to nearly 10,000. There has also been a 15% increase in suicide by British young people age fifteen to twenty-four.

To change our viewpoint just a bit:

Another part of the argument for suicide rests on the teaching of Martin Heidegger, the German philosopher, who pointed out the vast difference there is between seeing life as a series of functions-leading-to-death and seeing it as a series of symbolic acts that lead to a symbolic death and to what we Christians call the Resurrection. The argument goes that many elderly people decide on rational suicide as a testimony to hope.

I am reminded of the suicide pact between Dr. Henry Pitney Van Dusen and his wife, Elizabeth. It should be said, from the pro-suicide viewpoint, that their suicide note can be taken as just such a statement of hope. Although I cannot see it that way myself, I am aware that many of their friends do so. And because their suicide note is not readily available to the general reader, I reprint it here so that the reader can come to his or her own conclusion:

To all friends and relations,
We hope that you will understand what we have done even though some of you will disapprove of it and some be disillusioned by it.

We have both had very full and satisfying lives. Pitney has worked hard and with great dedication for the church. I have had an adventurous and happy life. We both had happy lives and our children have crowned this happiness.

But since Pitney had his stroke five years ago, we have not been able to do any of the things we want to do and are able to do, and my arthritis is much worse. There are too many helpless old people who without modern medicinal care would have died, and we feel God would have allowed them to die when their time had come.

Nowadays it is difficult to die. We feel that this way we are taking will become more usual and acceptable as the years pass. Of course, the thought of our children and our grandchildren makes us sad, but we still feel that this is the best way and the right way to go. We are both increasingly weak and unwell and who would want to die in a Nursing Home?

We are not afraid to die.

We send you all our love and gratitude for your wonderful support and friendship.

"O Lamb of God that takest away the sins
    of the world
Have mercy upon us
O Lamb of God that takest away the sins
    of the world
Grant us thy peace."

Elizabeth B. Van Dusen
Henry P. Van Dusen

Again, in trying to describe the case for suicide, I must point out that Linnea Pearson and Ruth Purtilo, in their book *Separate Paths: Why People End Their Lives,* believe that it is important to recall that the Van Dusens died *together.* It is generally true that most suicides die alone because they feel alone. But the Van Dusens acted within the context of their marriage, feeling that their children and grandchildren were quite close to them. The authors of this book then raise the question: "Can suicide be seen as acceptable if it is done within the context of human caring and community?" They go on to say, "Their tone was one of pilgrims setting out into an unknown but promising direction. They were leading the way for many who might otherwise lack the courage or insight to make this choice."[4]

To be sure, as I have said before, there has been considerable controversy over the suicide pact of the Van Dusens. But whichever side one takes on this particular incident, it cannot be forgotten that Henry Pitney Van Dusen was for many years the president of one of the most prestigious and influential theological seminaries in the entire world. He was held in great respect by the theologians of all branches of Christendom. Perhaps it is not too much to say that it was his suicide that forced the theologians to face a long-neglected aspect of their tradition.

In its February 26, 1975, edition, *The New York Times* carried this comment about the Van Dusens:

The manner in which the Van Dusens pursued the issue, friends recall, was in keeping with their thorough and frank approach to major concerns. Many friends were accustomed to weighing the merits of suicide without macabre overtones. Consistent with customary parliamentary procedure, a hallmark of Presbyterianism and Dr. Van Dusen's own particular style, various viewpoints were heard and considered.[5]

The proponents of suicide will say that it is necessary to examine the suicide letter left behind. They would say that the most striking thing about it is the final prayer—a traditional part of the communion service. That is, this is taken to mean that for the Van Dusens the meaning of communion is that in all the brokenness of life, Christians are brought together in Christ. Whatever weakness we have and display, through Christ we are brought to the power of God—and the peace of God. Hence, their calm and deliberate statement: We are not afraid to die.

But perhaps it is Norman Cousins who has raised the ultimate question asked by the pro-suicide adherents: In his *Saturday Review* column of June 14, 1975, commenting on the death of the Van Dusens, he asked, "Why are so many people more readily appalled by an unnatural form of dying than by an unnatural form of living?"

Another part of the same question, from that point of view, is seen in the words of the well-known Christian martyr Dietrich Bonhoeffer. Man, he says, is a creature of God, but he is not an animal. And the difference lies in the God-given ability to make a free choice in every major decision that life requires.

> Man, unlike the beasts, does not carry his life as a compulsion which he cannot throw off. He is free either to accept his life or to destroy it. Unlike the beasts, man can put himself to death of his own free will. An animal is one with the life of his body, but man can distinguish himself from the life of his body. The freedom in which man possesses his bodily life requires him to accept this life freely, and at the same time it directs his attention to what lies beyond this bodily life and compels him to regard the life of his body as a gift that is to be preserved and a sacrifice that is to be offered. Only because a man is free to choose death can he lay down the life of his body for some higher good. Without freedom to sacrifice one's life in death, there can be no freedom towards God, there can be no human life.[6]

In this connection, the proponents of this view would say that it is just this idea that Jesus was expressing when he said, "No one takes my life from me, but I lay it down of my own accord. I have power to lay it down and I have power to take it again; this charge I have received from my Father" (John 10:18).

In the book *Separate Paths* referred to above by Pearson and Purtilo, it is suggested that our entire concept of suicide might be altered if the verb "commit" was thought of as "to give in trust or charge; to entrust" (as in "to commit one's soul to God") rather than "to do" (as in "to commit a crime"). They say: "This concept tends to elevate the act of suicide to that of sacrifice—offering up one's life to God—not the *taking* of a life, but the *giving* of a life."[7]

The argument from the pro-suicide viewpoint would go something like this: The element of choice is essential. One does not *give* unless he or she is free to give. And if all of life is seen as a covenant with God, as a temporary loan from God, then one must be free to choose when and how that covenant is to be completed, that loan to be repaid. Which means, of course, that one must choose while one is still capable of choosing. It is surely the ability to choose that separates humans from animals. "So God created man in his own image; in the image of God he created him; male and female he created them" (Gen. 1:27 NEB).

And so those who argue from this viewpoint would probably say that the pastor who called himself "Hopeless Case" was not mindful of this distinction when he said that God had "condemned him to live." God, they would say, condemns us neither to life nor death. Both are gifts, covenants, loans.

Canon P. R. Baelz, now canon of Durham Cathedral in England and recently canon of Christ Church and regius professor of moral and pastoral theology at Cambridge University, sums up this view in a succinct paragraph in a recent essay:

> The dialectic of freedom and dependence, of action and passion, of doing and suffering, is far more subtle than has been suggested. Certainly in death there is a final passion, and for victory over death we must wait upon God. But does this necessarily

mean that we must in all circumstances wait upon the course of events which we call dying? If it is certain that the natural course of events will result in my being robbed of my proper humanity through the onset of pains greater than I can bear or the degradations of imbecility, is a decision to end my life before nature does it for me incompatible with my acknowledging my ultimate and total dependence on God? If my disintegration as a human being occurs before death, is there still any sense in speaking of either action or passion, self-determination or waiting on God?[8]

What I have written above, then, seems to me to be a fair summary of the essential argument that is being made by those who speak of rational suicide. I concede that these men and women are sincere and honest in their interpretation of what they conceive to be the Christian viewpoint on this subject. But I cannot agree.

Chapter 2

Suicide and Mystical-Psychic Experience

"There is no death! What seems so is transition;
This life of mortal breath Is but a suburb of the life
elysian, Whose portal we call Death."
                              —LONGFELLOW, *"Resignation"*

What does a close encounter with death say to the person who has attempted suicide and returned to life remembering the experience? What is his or her attitude afterward?

Dr. Raymond A. Moody, Jr., is popular for his contribution to the study of death or near-death experiences. In his book *Reflections on Life After Life,* which is a sequel to his best-seller, *Life After Life,* there is a chapter on suicide.

According to Dr. Moody, all his subjects reject suicide as an answer for the problems of life. They report that life must have a purpose. None of the subjects want to repeat their experience because, in some powerful way, it taught them that suicide was fraught with a penalty. Part of the penalty would be to "witness the suffering on the part of others that this act would cause."[1]

One man told Dr. Moody: "If I were to commit suicide I would be throwing God's gift back in his face ... and killing somebody else would be interfering with God's purpose for that individual."[2] His research into this strange aspect of "dying" showed that all agreed that attempted suicide solved nothing. More important, whatever they were trying to escape from was still there. One subject said that her condition, which caused her to attempt suicide, just kept repeating itself. Another man told Dr. Moody: "I will die naturally next time ... so much needs to be done while you're here. And when you die it's eternity."[3] Having met Dr. Moody, shared the platform with him, and spent hours with him on an airplane from Montreal, I can respect his research and his further contribution to the study of after-death states.

"Do Suicide Survivors Report Near-Death Experiences?" This was the title of a paper presented at the American Psychological Association conference in Montreal, Canada, September 4, 1980. The authors, Kenneth Ring and Stephen Franklin, of the Department of Psychology at the University of Connecticut, conducted interviews with thirty-six persons who had been close to death as a result of a suicide attempt. The findings were different from those reported by Dr. Moody's suicide cases. In the descriptions researched by Drs. Ring and Franklin, not one person reported an unpleasant experience. This does not necessarily mean to me, as a priest, that suicide can be accepted in society. Since death did not occur, we do not know what would be the "after shock," if there is one, on their consciousness, even though most described a "near-death" in this report as "I felt good; peaceful; relaxed; mellow; nice; calm; free; pleasant; inspired; warm; safe; out of my body; wonderful; clear; drifting; lights; floating; pulled back; blackness; falling; speed; suction; colors; moving down a tunnel; meeting a deceased loved one and voices."

Drs. Ring and Franklin say: "Near-death research can never settle the question of whether there is a hell anymore than its findings can prove the existence of an afterlife as such. Even if we do assume that NDEs represent the transition into death, we cannot say what the *eventual* fate of successful suicides might be; we can only recount the initial experiences of those who *fail.*"

Something of an attempt at this type of research appeared in 1961 when Dr. Karlis Osis was head of the Division of Research for the Parapsychology Foundation. Dr. Osis produced a monograph called *Deathbed Observations by Physicians and Nurses.* Questionnaires were sent to five thousand physicians and to five thousand nurses; 640 were returned. The results indicated that people indeed experience encounters with another reality and experiments with death began to take on a laboratory significance. Recent efforts to discredit such investigations include the work of Dr. Ernest Rodin, associated with the Lafayette Clinic in Detroit, Michigan. His theory about such efforts as Dr. Moody's and others' is simply that those who are ill suffer what he calls "fleeting insanity that accompanies the loss of oxygen to the brain" in what he terms "toxic psychosis."[4]

Dr. Moody continues with his work in disregard to Dr. Rodin, and so we are left with a vast background of mystical and paranormal experiences down through the ages in which there are patterns of truth and direction. Dr. Moody's points are well taken in his research, although he does not endorse or make ethical judgments or theological arguments. He does tell us of countless interviews carefully researched. The evidence for a transcendental dimension for the existence of life-after-life grows daily with the accumulated experiences of people in all facets of life.

One of the most amazing and profound "out of the body" experiences was that of psychiatrist Dr. George C. Ritchie, of Richmond, Virginia. He was pronounced dead on the morning of December 20, 1943. Nine minutes later he returned to life. He had double lobar pneumonia, and at the time he was a private in the army. A soldier was assigned to prepare his body for the morgue. The ward soldier thought he saw a slight movement, and he ran to the doctor. A hypodermic of adrenalin was then given directly into the heart muscle, and Dr. Ritchie, as the title of his book infers, made a "return from tomorrow."[5]

I have spoken with Dr. Ritchie about his experience and heard him present his lecture several times while engaging him to speak on various occasions. In regard to his recall of what happened during his "death," he relates: "If you think you can commit suicide without cost you're wrong."

Dr. Ritchie was not an attempted suicide, but his out-of-the-body travels showed him levels or realms of the departed that must be considered unique and perceptive. He says, "There is universe work lost when a suicide occurs and the suicide becomes an earthbound soul until he learns the cost of taking his own life. He must remain present to understand the unhappiness that he has brought into the lives of others and until that lesson is learned, he cannot continue into other realms."[6] In his encounter with "people" who had died by their own hand, Dr. Ritchie received an answer to a question asked about people who kept pleading with others who were living who could not hear them. He was told, "They are suicides, chained to every consequence of their act."[7]

Although there have been numerous cases of out-of-the-body experiences, there is further need for suicide research material. If a preponderance of evidence leads to a "don't do it" theory, then such research will serve a great purpose. Perhaps one of the best-known early researchers in out-of-the-body or "astral" travel is Great Britain's Robert Crookall, a geologist and a former demonstrator in botany at the University of Aberdeen. His special research has brought him esteem in the field of psychic research. In his book *The Supreme Adventure* (London: James Clarke & Co., Ltd., 1961), he approaches the suicide as an "earthbound" having rejected the great opportunities of earth life to escape what is their bounden duty and service to mankind. Crookall sees these unfortunate entities as those who have rejected opportunity or "life itself." Crookall says they survive, and even though they have destroyed the body, they take their problems with them. He sees the physical body in this life as a "steadying, initiative-providing body charged with a vitality that is prematurely dissipated." (p. 32) His conclusions regarding earthbound personalities is summed up in the phrase "pray for me."

Even though the history of spiritualism is fraud run amuck, literature abounds with references to the danger of suicide. The famous psychic William Stainton Moses, an Anglican clergyman in 1873 who was noted for his books such as *Spirit Teachings,* said that "nothing is more dangerous than for souls to be rudely severed from their bodily habitation, and to be launched into spirit-life with angry passions stirred, and revengeful feelings dominant ... it is a barbarous ignorance of the conditions of life and progress in the hereafter. ..."[8] He infers that such conditions of death provide for influences on earth that are far from healthy. If this is true, what happens as a result of legalized murder such as the putting to death of criminals? Are we really rid of them? And what are we to say concerning all the aborted souls?

Allen Kardec, once called the father of spiritism in France, was a controversial psychic. He produced many books including a textbook on spiritistic philosophy called *The Spirits' Book.* Much of this material is of a simplistic nature, but the subject of suicide is treated with disdain. In a question-and-answer session with the beyond, the question "Has a man the right to dispose of his life?" is posed. The answer is a firm no. The right belongs only to God, and anyone who commits the crime "contravenes the providential ordering which sent him into the earthly life."[9] According to Kardec even if one commits suicide to escape the disgrace of a wrongdoing, the "fault is not effaced . . . for . . . he who has had the courage to do wrong should have the courage to bear the consequences of his wrongdoing."[10]

In regard to the knowledge of our own forthcoming death by a disease or some prolonged illness, the message is "It is always wrong not to await the moment of dissolution appointed by God. Besides, how can a man tell whether the end of his life has really come, or whether some unexpected help may not reach him at what he supposes to be his last moment?"[11]

When I was a student in seminary, a storekeeper near my dormitory committed suicide after his wife died. He could not live without her. The morning after the tragedy my professor made a comment about the incident: "He only proved that he loved his wife more than he loved God." I have thought about that many times. Kardec has a statement about just such a situation when a person enacts the self-kill with the hope of rejoining his loved one. He states: "Instead of being reunited to the object of their affection, those who have made this sad mistake find themselves separated, and for a very long time, from the being they hoped to rejoin; for God cannot recompense, by the granting of a favour, an act which is at once a proof of moral cowardice, and an insult offered to Himself in distrusting His Providence."[12]

The one statement by Kardec that seems to reaffirm some of the current research in after-death states is that of disappointment. The consequences would not be the same in all cases, but there are consequences. He seems to make sense when he reminds the reader that the "consequences of violent death are, first the prolongation of the mental confusion which usually follows death, and next, the illusion which usually follows death, and next, the illusion which causes a spirit, during a longer or shorter period, to believe himself to be still living in the earthly life."[13] There are also the problems of the delay in progress, which may be denied, and, as Kardec sensibly portrays, the act of suicide being contrary to the law of nature. In other words, no benefit is gained by suicide but rather it results in prolonged efforts by the deceased to free themselves from what they tried to escape from. The last state is worse than the first.

Charles L. Tweedale, an English vicar interested in psychic research, wrote *Man's Survival After Death.* His research proclaims the same results about suicide. Whatever evidence he found for life after death in regard to suicide, there was always the emphasis on need for prayer for those who have taken their lives. Prayer for the departed is most important, especially for suicides.

In my opinion, Theosophy goes beyond other groups in detailing the effects of self-destruction. I once knew a theosophical scholar named Alvin Boyd Kuhn. He was a fascinating man, and as a young Episcopal theological student, Kuhn was the last person my professors would expect me to have lunch with. His insights were profound in many respects, and he wrote books, including one called *Theosophy* that was part of a series in American religions. The philosophy states that the suicide must live in a "near-earthly existence" for the term of his or her natural life. And, interestingly enough, he or she is tempted to enjoy life again through psychics or a sort of vampiristic obsession. In this sense Dr. Ritchie also observed the deceased alcoholics trying to quench their thirst through the living drinkers. They were dead, but they still had their problems because the problems were not solved on earth while living. According to Theosophy, "Each one's heaven is determined by the capacities for spiritual enjoyment developed on earth. Only the spiritual senses survive."[14] This is not the case with suicides in their efforts of premature death.

Theosophist Annie Besant, in her book *The Ancient Wisdom,* takes the same position—that sudden death in any form causes problems. But, in the case of those who are spiritually minded, accidental death is slept out, so to speak, with no great difficulty. One thinks of that phrase in the ancient Litany of delivery from "murder and from sudden death."[15] In other cases such as suicide, they are "entangled in the final scene of earth life . . . and unaware that they have lost the physical body."[16] Besant writes, "A suicide will repeat automatically the feelings of despair and fear which preceded his self-murder, and go through the act and the death-struggle time after time with ghastly persistence."[17]

In an interesting booklet called *States After Death,* the fate of suicides is further discussed. "The astral shells of suicides and executed criminals are the most coherent and longest lived. . . . In the case of a suicide, the unhappy being revolts against the trials of life and kills the body, but finds itself precisely as much alive mentally as before."[18] This approach presents us with a kind of half-dead state in which one may, according to Theosophy, then be attracted to mediums. They claim that if mediums knew this they would be less motivated to wanting "communication" with the so-called dead. Communication is the most controversial of all aspects of the psychic or paranormal side of personality and still the great question in psychic research. Again it is stated that the actual natural life term must be waited out, whether it is one year or fifty years. The literature affirms that appointed life time. We must not prematurely or premeditatedly interrupt the life clock.

I am not endorsing the doctrine of spiritualism, Theosophy, or any other group, but am stating simply that there is a ring of truth about these insights in regard to the perplexing problem of self-destruction. There is also a preponderance of evidence that keeps saying *don't do it!*

Dr. Ian Stevenson is perhaps the most learned scholar in the world on the subject of reincarnation. He is a scholar and a recognized expert whose research is respected. He has accumulated more cases for "claimed memory" of former lives than any other person. Whether one believes in reincarnation is not the issue in this book, but if it actually occurs, then it is again one of the ways we may survive. It is not taught by the modern Church. It does imply that survival exists, and that is the issue. Do we survive death? If we do, then we must contend with more than mere ethics or rights in regard to suicide.

In some cases investigated by Dr. Stevenson the subject who claims to have lived before affirms that in a former life he committed suicide. In this life those same fears haunt him as a carry-over waiting to be enacted again. Naturally, the question of heredity versus reincarnation has been thoroughly considered by Dr. Stevenson and, in the end, we cannot be sure. But the evidence for claimed memory is indeed very strong in so many other instances than just a few cases where suicide has been a factor. Dr. Stevenson's works are worthy of study, especially *Twenty Cases Suggestive of Reincarnation.*

One of the most interesting approaches to reincarnation and suicide is presented by Manly P. Hall, a writer of philosophy and religion. His Philosophical Research Society, Inc. has been turning out material since 1934, and Hall, himself, has delivered over seven thousand lectures in the United States and abroad, and has written countless books and articles. He writes of suicide in his book *Reincarnation: The Cycle of Necessity.* Hall says, "The psychic toxin of suicide, however, enters into the fabric of the entity, and it affects the normalcy of the next personality."[19] He claims that the self-destructive tendency in those who fear life must be altered by spiritual education. Like other teachers he accepts the theory that those who self-destruct are caught in a halfway position in the afterlife. His point is well taken about the "college boy who commits suicide through boredom with the world of which he is a part [who] has comparatively little after-death consciousness. He has developed neither his emotions nor his thoughts to a degree of maturity. He remains earthbound until the time when his death would have normally occurred, and then his personality is rapidly dissolved as there is little possibility of transferring rational experience to the entity."[20] He uses the illustration of the play *Outward Bound* by Sutton Vane, in which the two suicides are called halfways. They cannot go forward or backward. They are cemented in a kind of fixed dimension.

Hall provides good insight about early Christians not being branded suicides simply because they chose their spiritual convictions rather than life under pagan rule—so they died as martyrs rather than abdicate truth. That is why we do not think of them as suicides in the same sense as the college boy who jumps out a window. Whether or not the martyrs ended up with the Lord any faster because they submitted to death is a question that cannot be answered. In any event, the point is made by Hall that life is not to be evaded, but to be lived. Hall believes that accidental death does not cause much trouble except that the personality may be temporarily earthbound because of the unexpected circumstances of death and the "intense physical attachment" to this life. He also claims that cremation helps to sever the ties between the physical realm and the spiritual.

The attitude of the Roman Catholic Church is firm on suicide. Burial is no longer denied, but there is an approach that may say, in unusual terms, what the Church thinks. The following case is an example: In 1949 Luigi Galafate, twenty-eight years old, climbed to the inner dome of St. Peter's Basilica. If you have been there you will remember a walkway. You can look down on the high altar. Above you is light streaming from the opening in the dome. It is the symbolic door to heaven. Its height is grand and awesome. Galafate proceeded to leap over the rail and plunged to his death. He landed near the high altar, where people were kneeling in prayer. This happened before in 1947. In 1949 a despondent Italian lawyer jumped to his death. The church considers such an act a desecration. To profane a holy place or disrupt the sacred atmosphere by a weird or vile act is a desecration. As a result, the basilica was reconsecrated.

The attitude toward a suicide in the basilica is one of disdain, but to reconsecrate St. Peter's Basilica is indeed an affirmation that suicide is condemned. The act of consecration of an altar or sacred place implies that there may be negative influences present as a result of the vile act.

In the Roman Ritual there is the Rite for Reconsecration of an altar. The prayer has within it a form of exorcism as if to say that anything earthbound or disruptive to the beauty and theme of spiritual unity must be protected. The prayer implores that kind of protection. This is the prayer for the holy water to be used in the re-blessing:

> God's creature, water, I cast out the demon from you in the name of God the Father, † and of the Son, † and of the Holy † Spirit. May you drive out Satan from the orders of the just, lest he lurk within the shadows of this church and this altar. And you, Lord Jesus Christ, pour out your Holy Spirit on this

church and altar, that those who worship you here may be rewarded in body and soul, that your name may be glorified among all nations, and the hearts of unbelievers be converted to you, and have no other God but you, the only true Lord, who is coming to judge both the living and the dead and the world by fire.

Amen.[21]

The service then proceeds until finally, "May this altar be sealed † and hallowed †; in the name of the Father, † and of the Son, † and of the Holy † Spirit. Peace be to you."[22]

Not only have the dome and high altar been the site of death, but also in 1979 a fifty-year-old Italian barber knelt in front of the tomb of Pope John XXIII, in the crypt, and shot himself. When Pope John Paul II was told of this, he immediately went to his private chapel to pray.

Pope Pius XII spoke out in 1958 on suicide by saying, "Life belongs to God, and no one may renounce it without committing a most serious sin. You understand we allude to all too many suicides attempted or committed in all cities and in all classes. . . . Try to do everything possible to impede this evil from growing. The fight against suicide belongs to the duties of a priest."[23]

Chapter 3

The Temptation of Death

"Death will tempt people with the promise of greater security than they can find in this lifetime —unless and until such time as we are able to teach man to accept his own destiny."
— DR. JOOST A. M. MEERLOO

In my pastoral work I have found that those who are prone to depression are most encouraged to consider their own deaths during holiday seasons. They believe others are happy while they feel sad. Christmas is a special time. Unless the real meaning of the season is well grounded in the consciousness, it can act as a catalyst for depression, loneliness, and self-deprecation. Contemplating the loss of a loved one on some special anniversary, or even some hymn in the atmosphere of a church service, can stir negative emotions.

One woman told me that since the death of her son twenty years ago, she cannot attend church. Church upsets her. She finds no comfort in a sanctified place because she has not discovered the basic understanding of the gospel message to sustain her. Her religious orientation is merely emotional. Instead of being uplifted, this type of person feeds on the negative. The negative, in turn, pulls her down. One parishioner's brother was killed. He was a priest. Up until his death she was a faithful member. She will not allow herself to face the atmosphere of a church service because she feels inside her that God let her down. Until we can enlarge our view of God and life, we will not be able to cope with what is only a surface affair with religion. The Jesus of the Gospels is not whom we are thinking of in these crisis situations.

E. L. Abel wrote *Moon Madness.* He refers to an article in *The American Journal of Psychiatry* by Dr. J. Oliven, in which it is reported that "more than half of the reported suicides for a particular period were found to have occurred at the time of the full moon."[1] He then cites a study done in the city of Chicago by Dr. S. A. Levinson that showed "there was a marked tendency for certain individuals to kill themselves around the new or full moon, rather than at some other time during the month."[2] The moon is not the cause, but indications are that there may be an influence on our moods; therefore, it is imperative to encourage right attitudes from the beginning in any suicidal type. The important thing is to develop in the patient a love of life. A story is told of the Swiss psychologist Carl Jung. He was not happy about the prospect of death during his final illness. He had a stern housekeeper, and when she left the room in his final moments, he gasped to his son: "Quick, help me out of bed before she comes back or she will stop me. I want to look at the sunset."[3]

A sense of beauty is a good protection. Many suicides take place in the night. Thoughts at night are very different from the day. "For in the night in which He [Jesus] was betrayed . . ."[4] The night surrounds us with its inky blackness. The night is a hidden time. At night we are left alone to our inmost thoughts. Night is a dangerous time. The day is flooded with light. Nothing is hidden. The sun streams forth with its rays of brilliance. As the sun illumines a room, so it illumines our thoughts. Sometimes, if we can wait out the night, we feel a new beginning. I have often told a person who has threatened suicide to "try to wait until tomorrow. It will be clearer then." The night tempts us in our thoughts of death.

Loss of faith is often accompanied by the temptation to die. In his booklet, *Am I Losing My Faith?*, William E. Hulme sees our faith being attacked from several corners—intellectual doubt, frustrations, emotions, guilts, and cultural patterns. He claims that we can get support for our faith through involvement. Most of all, we can encourage faith by involvement with people concerned about "the way of Christ."[5] One should not neglect the role of counseling in our lives. We can talk with others to help avoid a crisis of belief.

The natural order of life demands that we must all face death. Certainly, it is central to the Christian faith. How we think of it and are taught about it determines our approach. I surmise that it is not handled well as a pulpit subject in today's churches. This may be a reason so many grasp at death as a doorway from the responsibility of living. They have a secret love affair with death, but not a sense of perception about what it involves. If they did, they would not use it unwisely. Death is fascinating in itself. It is complicated. It is mysterious. It is certain. It will one day call our name. To pursue this feeling, if one is touched by it, is more difficult than the mere rejection of survival on the ground that "I believe only what I see." In the Christian religion, the future church and our own ongoing consciousness rest in the Resurrection account. But we also have the teaching that this future life begins now and is not something we are merely waiting for. To sense our purpose here is to overcome death and see that life here is just as valid and productive and that we are called to serve. What does a suicide serve? It serves itself. There is nothing to serve in self-afflicted death. If a man's religion has not given him a genuine confidence in a future life that begins now and makes it a reality for him, then it has failed to do what it should.

In Arthur Miller's great play, *"Death of a Salesman,"* there is a moment on the stage when the wife of Willy Loman, the worn-out salesman, speaks out against the events that have brought Willy to hopelessness and suicide. She says, "When things like this happen people have got to pay attention. A man can't come into the world with nothing and go out with nothing. A man has to add up to something." The wisdom of the ages, the great teachers, and the Christian Church are saying that you do add up to something. How dare we contradict the centuries and take the matter into our own hands by calling death upon ourselves?

If the temptation of death is near you, then try to think of yourself as more than bodily chemistry. You do stand in the cosmic scheme of things "a little lower than the angels, and crownedst him with glory and honor ..." (Heb. 2:7). In you, God is seen. God will not be seen in a death by suicide. Loved ones will suffer pain inflicted by the victim. Years from now the suicide will be remembered without smiles. Loved ones will always be wondering about that person. Their children's children will be told how the suicide could not cope with life, yet these children are to go on living without an example for living. Their sons and daughters will not be speaking of their demise and will hold that to themselves as a blight.

That is exactly what I have seen with each family that has experienced it. Even a clergyman whom I know whose father committed suicide never speaks of his father. There is no desire for public memory. It is as if the person left nothing because he or she abandoned everyone and everything. It is as though the person had never lived. If death should tempt you, draw upon whatever faith you have. Think of those who have tried to guide you. Try to remember someone important in your life. Think of someone who was once proud of you. Think of someone you have admired. Think of something that you heard or read that inspired you. Think of the possible consequences stated in another section of this book. I am not overly concerned with treatment for those who remain. They go on. The emphasis of this book is not just for those in grief because of a suicide. This book is concerned with you, or those you know or love because they have given thought to taking their life. Most everyone I encounter, in regard to this subject, has admitted to thinking of suicide, at least once, when the chips (as they say) were down.

Your goal, as a result of simple faith in the divine purpose both here and in the hereafter, is based on a faith commitment to God. You cannot change God, however you wish to interpret that word. You cannot manipulate God. Yes, everyone that dies will survive. This will occur automatically, according to definite laws of the unseen. How will they survive?

Jesus tells us in his account of the many mansions. He teaches that there are many levels or mansions, as he calls them, within which we shall take our place—the atheist, the degenerate, the dope addict, the alcoholic, the saint, the churchgoer, and the non-church-goer. But those who strive, who carry their cross, who follow, who live with him mentally and spiritually while on the path of the earthly life, will attain the highest possible levels. I believe that there are levels of consciousness, and the highest is perfect freedom, or as it is called "Heaven." This is not a physical place with golden roads and silver trees but a state of Being, where, as whole persons and conscious beings, we shall be in harmony with the universe.

I believe that if you commit suicide, you will not achieve any level of quality or clarity. It may well be that suicide can induce a conscious hell more closely akin to being lost or submerged in confusion and disorientation. That in itself would be a form of hell unlike the fundamentalist version, but yet, a hell where the mind is in torment. This is the basis of prayer for the so-called dead. Prayer heals, uplifts, and clears the consciousness of the deceased that they may move on into realms of light, rather than disorientation. One cannot begin to pray for the departed unless there is something to pray for. We pray because they do survive and grow: "He may go from strength to strength, in the life of perfect service, in thy heavenly kingdom . . ."6

When you are tempted to consider unnatural death, it is not the death Jesus speaks about. Jesus' efforts were to help us attain the highest levels of being and, above all, to attain a state with him: "Where I am, there ye may be also" (John 14:3).

*If—If—*you commit suicide, you will not be fulfilling the teaching of the Master. He indicates in his teaching that we must do our part on earth and complete the process that he set in motion. No one will learn anything from you if you self-destruct. They can only learn from your life in service to others. As a suicide you have nothing to teach, and that is why one must also consider the role of Judas. He left nothing behind but darkness. Jesus is telling us the truth, and Judas is a negative in the midst of positives.

The method of development taught by Jesus was not to absent ourselves from life. The mission was laid out for us to help change the consciousness of the world so that we could find the Christ within ourselves. This is the same thing the saints discovered. You may be critical of all that is clerical, but have you the will and the desire to adopt the higher life for yourself? If so, then you will find no room for suicide nor will you adopt a method to encourage others. The people cited in this book who have killed themselves were educated and uneducated. What did not unfold in them, you must try to unfold in yourself. To begin with, we are all spiritual. We are born that way. Birth, life, and death are all spiritual. The problem in life is to become aware of our natural spirituality. The potential is there. All the great teachers of wisdom have tried to awaken this potential in human consciousness.

Each one's task in life is to be less sidetracked by the roads that lead to oblivion. Money, position, fame, addiction of all kinds, or family problems will not give the answers. This is not to imply that money, position, and fame are to be shunned, but rather to be used properly. Think about this group:

In 1923, a group of the world's most successful financiers met at the Edgewater Beach Hotel in Chicago. Present were:

The president of the largest independent steel company.

The president of the largest utility company.

The greatest wheat speculator.

The president of the New York Stock Exchange.

A member of the President's cabinet.

The greatest "bear" in Wall Street.

The president of the Bank of International Settlement.

The head of the world's greatest monopoly.

What had happened to these eight men twenty-five years later?

The president of the largest steel company, Charles Schwab, lived on borrowed money the last five years of his life and died "broke."

The utility company president, Samuel Insull, died virtually in exile.

The greatest wheat speculator, Arthur Patton, died abroad, insolvent.

The president of the New York Stock Exchange, Richard Whitney, had served a term in Sing Sing Prison.

The member of the President's cabinet, Albert Fall, was pardoned from prison so he could die at home.

The greatest "bear" in Wall Street, Jesse Livermore, committed suicide.

The president of the Bank of International Settlement, Leon Frazier, committed suicide.

The head of the world's greatest monopoly, Ivan Kreuger, committed suicide.

All these men had learned about life, but not one of them had learned how to live it.

Source unknown

We have traveled a long way from an unhealthy approach to death and dying in our society. My hope is that the future will encourage an even more stable approach that will somehow defeat the proponents of suicide as a way of dying. Suicide is so far from a healthy Christian—or even non-Christian—answer to life that it is an insult to the very gift of life itself.

When I think of a healthy view of Christian

death in natural ways, I think of the Reverend Dr. W. Cosby Bell. He once wrote a book entitled *If a Man Die*. After the manuscript was completed Dr. Bell, who was at the time a professor at the Virginia Theological Seminary, suffered a heart attack. When told that he was dying, he sent the following message to his seminary students:

> Tell the boys that I've grown surer of God every year of my life, and I've never been so sure as I am right now. Why, it's all so! ... it's a fact ... it's a dead certainty! I'm so glad to find that I haven't the least shadow of shrinking or uncertainty. I've been preaching and teaching these things all my life, and I'm so much interested to find that all we've been believing and hoping is so. I've always thought so and now that I'm right up against it, I know.
>
> Tell them I say good-bye ... they've been a joy to me. I've had more than any man that ever lived, and life owes me nothing. I've had work I loved, and I've lived in a beautiful place among congenial friends. I've had love in its highest form and I've got it forever ... I can see now that death is just the smallest thing ... just an incident ... that it means nothing. There's no real break ... God is there ... and life ... and all that really counts in life ... goes on.[7]

Because death is mysterious and there are so many hard places in life, many people are tempted to try to explore death as a way out of their troubles. In fact, even the letter written by Dr. Bell, which I have just quoted, could be taken by some as an encouragement to meet death. *But* Dr. Bell was not engaged in the act of suicide when he wrote that letter. He was demonstrating the blessing of God upon a life of service.

The temptation of death is false, and it is filled with self-deception.

Chapter 4

The Ways and Means of Suicide

▰▰▰▰▰▰▰▰

"Some indeed have been so affectedly vain as to counterfeit immortality, and have stolen their death in hopes to be esteemed immortal."
—SIR THOMAS BROWNE

Alarming statistics reveal that suicide is now the third leading cause of death among the American youth. Any clergyman who has had to deal with this problem knows the trauma and frustration of trying to talk a person out of self-destruction. My own approach goes something like this: "Did you ever think that if you destroyed your God-given body that you might still be conscious? Think about that. Think about all the research in the study of consciousness and ask yourself, If I kill myself what am I killing? Suppose you did this and suddenly you were still you, but without your physical vehicle. Do you think that you would still have problems? That would be a terrible fate. Maybe you would have to work it out anyway, and the road that you have avoided would only become more difficult."

There are many other take-off points, but this has a religious connotation. Also the question must be posed whether or not the victim believes in life after death. If the potential suicide is for the purpose of going to a better place, then a different approach should be made about why we are here and the purposes we may not fulfill, or the pain we leave behind for those who have loved us and tried to help. If it is for the purpose of annihilation, then we must convince the person that there is no annihilation, only survival and what it might be like. This was my attitude toward a young man who attempted suicide twice. First he threatened to jump from a high place. Second he hooked himself to the television set. Instead of killing himself, he killed the television set. It shorted out in a puff of smoke. This young man is still alive. His condition was aggravated by the use of drugs.

Many youth suicides are drug-induced—a condition whereby, after using a chemical substance, the "gears", so to speak, do not return to normal and the act is committed as if encouraged by a false condition in the biochemical system. This happened in my city to the daughter of a prominent radiologist. The young lady left the family room, went to the garage, and doused herself with gasoline. Upon returning to the family she said, "Look what I have done!" She ignited herself and proceeded to go up in flames before her parents' eyes. This drug-related death is not an isolated case in these addictive times. This young lady represents a kind of dissociated type that can cope with day-to-day life, but was somehow motivated to kill herself in a kind of fantasy mentality. The same was true in 1969 for the daughter of show business personality Art Linkletter. Diane Linkletter jumped six floors to her death. Her father said, "It wasn't suicide because she wasn't herself. It was murder. She was murdered by the people who manufacture and sell LSD." Well said, but the fact remains she did it to herself.

With or without drugs, 10 to 15 percent of America's youth have thought seriously about suicide or have attempted to kill themselves. The rate is rising especially among the ten-to-fourteen age bracket, as well as the fifteen-to-twenty-four age bracket. It does not take much to cause the problem. Eddie Seidel, Jr., is a good example. He jumped two hundred feet from a bridge because the television program "Battlestar Galactica" was canceled. The program, he claimed, was his whole life.

Education has little to do with suicide. William D. Pawley, former ambassador to Brazil, shot himself. Robert M. Hurt, lecturer in economics at Princeton University, shot himself. Dr. Conrad Berens, professor at Columbia University, shot himself. Merriman Smith, White House correspondent, shot himself. John Berryman, Pulitzer Prize winner, jumped off a bridge.

Show people have their own special heartaches over suicide. Walter Winchell, Jr., shot himself. Hollywood producer Rex Carlton shot himself. The son of William Powell was found in the shower, stabbed to death. He left a note that said, "Things are not good here. I am going where things are better." Charlie Swift, the sportscaster, shot himself after leaving a note to tell his wife how much he loved her. Jonathan Hale, Mr. Dithers in "Blondie," shot himself. Sammee Tong, who acted in "Bachelor Father," took sleeping pills. He wrote, "I have taken my own life. No one is to blame." Phil Ochs, the folksinger, hanged himself. Jennifer Jones's daughter leaped twenty-two stories to her death. The playwright Max Wylie, who was also executive editor of the television program "Wide, Wide World," shot himself. Chris Chubbuck shot herself on television: "In keeping with Channel 40's policy of having the news first, you are going to see another first—an attempted suicide."

Charles Boyer's son was an apparent suicide while the father himself was later listed as a drug suicide. Georgia Skelton, the former wife of Red Skelton, shot herself. Who can forget the publicity surrounding the suicide of Freddie Prinze of the television show "Chico and the Man." He shot himself in the head. The song "Where Is the Love" was written by Donny Hathaway, who dove thirteen stories out of a New York hotel. Actor Gig Young shot himself; Jenny Arness, daughter of James Arness, died of an overdose; and Gregory Peck's son, Jonathan, shot himself. One of my favorite actors, George Sanders, took an overdose and left this note: "Because I am bored and have lived enough."

My interest in stage magic prompts me to think of magicians who have presented great mysteries, but could not handle the mystery of life. Dante the Magician had an associate called Danton who could not take the rejection of a possible large show as a second unit of the "Great Dante." In response to this, Danton drove his car off a cliff. Ted Annenemen was a marvelous mentalist, but his own mental problems drove him to breathe gas from the kitchen oven and die. A magician named Satan blew his brains out in Philadelphia; the famous writer William Linsay Gresham, who wrote the book *Houdini: The Man Who Walked Thru Walls,* committed suicide by taking sleeping pills. Even the family of the "Great Houdini" could not escape the problem of suicide. Houdini's brother, Leopold, jumped to his death from a rooftop.

As one magician told me, "They weren't cowards. What they did took real guts." It may take guts, but the real seriousness is expressed by G. K. Chesterton: "The man who kills a man kills a man. The man who kills himself kills all men. As far as he is concerned, he wipes out the world."

Suicide is no respecter of position or accomplishment. It has happened to those in all walks of life, including the clergy. In 1975 the associate pastor of the First United Methodist Church of Fort Lauderdale, Florida, hanged himself in the church attic. He did not leave a note, but his wife said, "He had a bad faculty for taking other people's problems unto himself to help them, but then he couldn't get rid of the problems himself. He just had that one problem too many he couldn't throw off."[1] The Reverend Franklin I. Sheeder also hanged himself in a New York hotel room. He had an honorary Doctor of Divinity degree and was national executive of the United Church of Christ. What Episcopal priest can forget the case of Bishop James A.

Pike's son? He shot himself to death in a $5.25-a-day room in the New York Hotel Hudson.

A priest friend was the rector in a church where two youths committed suicide, in 1969, as a protest against the Vietnam War. Joan Fox and Craig Badiali were both seventeen years old. Theirs was a kind of romanticized death in which both were involved in high school politics. They used a vacuum cleaner hose attached to a car exhaust that went through the floorboard. Dr. Louis Riegert, New Jersey's Camden County Medical Examiner, read the twenty-four notes left to family and friends. He said: "They felt that by taking their lives, people who lived after them would appreciate their own lives. . . . They were somehow trying to prove that life is wonderful and meaningful . . . and they took their own lives to prove it." Their priest was so shocked by this tragedy that he himself had a nervous breakdown and attempted suicide by trying to drive his car into a pole on a major highway. His emotional life was further damaged by what was unfairly written about him in a book called *Craig and Joan.*

In 1962 the Vatican radio broadcast a plea to help prevent suicides. It reminded everyone that "in the scheme of creation, all those who are born into this world are destined to eternal life, and this life on earth is the phase in which they can reach their aim in obedience to the laws of God."[2]

Suicide is contempt for life, and when clergy take the laws of God into their own hands, it is even more serious, as in the case of the Reverend Dr. and Mrs. Henry Pitney Van Dusen, which I have mentioned before. Dr. Van Dusen was former president of Union Theological Seminary. Both he and his wife saw suicide as a way out with dignity. Mrs. Van Dusen took an overdose of pills and died. Dr. Van Dusen's overdose did not do the job and he lived. It was a bizarre case. He later died, but their letter stated, "Nowadays, it is difficult to die. We feel this way we are taking will become more usual and acceptable as the years pass." Their deaths took place in 1975. She died on January 29, and he died two weeks later in a Belle Meade, New Jersey, clinic. When he swallowed the pills, he did not digest them and vomited. Acting out a kind of sacrifice, their letter ends with a prayer: "O Lamb of God, that takest away the sins of the world, grant us Thy peace." Dr. John C. Bennett, who succeeded Dr. Van Dusen and who is now retired, said, "Knowing the circumstances, I think they did the right thing."

One clergyman who would agree is the Reverend Dr. Warren Briggs. He told a reporter for the Los Angeles *Times* that "reverence for life includes the right to die with dignity." Briggs believes that there should be suicide crisis clinics. After examination you could be helped to prepare your own death. The United Methodist clergyman addressed a conference on suicide in San Diego, California, where he said that "suicides in the Bible are not criticized."

One can only ponder if nuclear physicist Paul C. Aebersold would have passed the test. He was connected with the invention of the cyclotron, and in 1967 in Maryland he jumped seventeen floors to his death. Would Donald Dickinson Williams have been helped by such a clinic? He worked on the

Early Bird Satellite System. In 1966 he shot himself, fully clothed, in his shower-bath. Would Grant Stockdale have faired any better? He once was ambassador to Ireland. In 1963 he dove thirteen floors from the DuPont Building in Miami, Florida. How about Henry Peterson, former mayor of my city, Woodbury, New Jersey. He walked to a nearby lake and shot himself. How about Frank Fish, a prominent well-to-do Christian citizen of my city? He ended his life with a bullet. What about James Stone, junior warden and treasurer of Incarnation Parish, Madison Avenue, New York. He threw himself out of a twelfth-story window. Perhaps the cofounder of the Masters Golf Tournament, Cliff Roberts, might not have shot himself. Can we, in any way, affirm suicide as a method of death with dignity? No. Is there dignity to the deaths of Ernest Hemingway, Hart Crane, Virginia Woolf, Vincent van Gogh, Hannibal, actor Bruce Lee, or Judas Iscariot?

Let us consider why Judas was numbered among the twelve Apostles. What is the message of Judas? He is not honored in any church. There are no statues to him. There is no holy day to commemorate his life. We do find Judas in Leonardo da Vinci's *Last Supper,* but look closely and you will see spilled salt in front of him. It projects a nervous man contemplating betrayal. As he betrays Jesus with a kiss, so he betrays all of life with his death. In so many ways, he was like the other Apostles, but something was missing in his personality structure. Judas is there as the supreme example of weakness in character. He commits the eternal wrong, both physically and spiritually. He is a traitor, not only to Jesus but also to life. Dante, the writer, makes Judas' eternal torment the greatest. In his portrayal of hell, he places Judas in the lowest circle. Judas' head is in the mouth of the Devil. We have no hint of what happened to the soul and consciousness of Judas, even though I have heard clergymen maintain that one day Jesus would rescue Judas and raise him up.

Judas' impairment, his wrong assessment of Jesus, his acceptance of the thirty pieces of silver, his clever manipulation of steering the leaders to Jesus, his subsequent emotional collapse and his guilt show us a man who was weak on all counts. Judas is there for a purpose, for our learning. He is the example we must not follow. Judas is the suicide of every person ever since. He is our rejection of the spiritual value of life itself. Judas is the incarnate rejection of the son of man who knew that one of the twelve Apostles would be used by lower forces to betray him. He is the supreme traitor. He was a double-minded man. Until the last, Jesus tried to bring Judas into the love of God. Jesus did not reject him nor did he expose him as a traitor, but He knew.

God is always trying to win us to himself even unto the last moment, before it is too late. It was the potential of the man that interested Jesus when he chose Judas. Jesus sees what can be. It is that potential which life provides that we must see in those we want to help who do consider suicide. No one is considered lost until the horrendous act is perpetrated upon the self. Is it any wonder that suicide is looked upon with such disdain by Christianity? How then can those today who represent Christ espouse such a doctrine?

In Jerusalem, in 1975, Israeli Supreme Court Justice Haim Cohen, a talmudic scholar, said to the International Congress on Suicide Prevention that "Judaism permits 'suicide' for the sake of the 'sanctification of God's Holy Name' such as King Saul falling upon his sword after defeat by the Philistines." Another speaker, Dominican Father Marcel Dubois, spoke about Jesus as a possible suicide. He said that Jesus was not a suicide, but "had offered his life to his Father for the salvation of mankind."[3] He added that "suicide on one's own authority is an unpardonable sin since God had given life to man and only God could rightly take it away." This then would also apply to the ongoing debate of euthanasia or mercy killing. (If you were ill and wanted to die, someone would then grant you that privilege and kill you. They assist you in your own suicide.)

In pastoral visits to hospitals I have often heard the weary and diseased say, "Just let me die." Yes, but not with assistance of pills, guns, flames, or open windows. I have assisted in natural death and can attest that people have also died calm and peaceful deaths. These people seem to have almost "walked over to the other side" and, at the moment of passing, have "seen" a loved one waiting to help. Those were the deaths with dignity. There is no dignity in suicide.

This is one reason why the proposed publication of the booklet *How to Commit Suicide,* by the British organization that promotes euthanasia called

Exit (The Society for the Right to Die with Dignity), was a dangerous plan. Legally prevented from publication, the book is now scheduled for print by the Scottish branch of Exit. They reject pain in life's plan and hold that there is to be no suffering. Like the new-thought groups or modern happy-time-all-the-time religions and philosophies, there is no cross in the life of these followers of the easy road—a road that may take one on a journey into darkness rather than light.

Like Raymond A. Moody, Jr., M.D., Elisabeth Kubler-Ross, M.D., has written widely about death and dying. In her book *Questions and Answers on Death and Dying,* she states that some people are just poor risks for facing death. They always live, she says, as if there were a physical tomorrow, and when they do not see tomorrow they lose control. The tomorrow they see is always related to this world. One of the truths about Christianity is that there is a spiritual tomorrow, and they lack that conviction. This is where even some Christian people fail. They want Easter but no Lent. How can you have an Easter without a Lent? The conviction of survival is essential to a proper spiritual understanding of the Jesus story. It is difficult to gain this at the crisis point. Therefore, with many, the crisis time is a time to leave—to run away—to escape. Death is that escape for the unschooled in Christian truths. Thus, it is easy to see how a person would prefer to end it all. The end means a final point. The journey is over. Like a movie, after you have sweated out the story, there is that final release phrase—The End.

Dr. Kubler-Ross makes her point when she says,

"Our goal should be not to take lives, but to help people to live until they die their natural deaths."[4] I would agree with Dr. Kubler-Ross when she says, "I don't think we should advertise suicide as being everyone's right."[5]

Death as escape - [ok critique ec]

Chapter 5

Guidance: Religion or Medicine?

"He who takes truth for his guide, and duty for his end, may safely trust to God's Providence to lead him aright."

—BLAISE PASCAL

In Cleveland, Tennessee, a thirty-year-old man carefully planned his own funeral. He chose his own casket and made his own arrangements. Hobart F. Green, Jr., then ran a hose from the exhaust pipe into his car. He turned on the engine. He died.

The song he chose for his funeral service was "Take Me Home, Country Roads."

An Episcopal priest told me that his senior warden did the same thing, using car exhaust. His directress of the Altar Guild took an overdose of drugs. A layman in his parish used a knife to end his life.

The priest had spent hours counseling his senior

warden. He thought the problem had been solved. But nothing seemed to help. Sometimes unusual approaches can prevent suicide. Sister of Mercy Bernadette Smyth opened beer cans while talking to Timothy Bishop, who was on a ledge of a twenty-three story building in Albany, New York. She said, "He got a charge out of the fact that I was popping beer cans for him." Finally, Timothy was rescued.

Counseling can have its problems regarding suicide. In Los Angeles, a couple was so distraught by their son's death that they issued a law suit against the church that tried to help him. The family was Roman Catholic. The boy went to a Protestant church for guidance, but later killed himself. The parents charged the church and the pastor with "wrongful death, negligence, outrageous conduct and clergy malpractice." The approach of the clergy to the subject of suicide spans the spectrum of the problem. One pastor wrote me and said: "I believe the increase in suicide in this country is the direct result of the fact that a major portion of our society has no sense of its individual worth to God, to others or to themselves. I, personally, see our nation's suicide problem as a condemnation of the church which has failed to get across the good news to those people most in need of it." An editor of a magazine on healing told me, "I believe that suicide is an abnormal reaction to the pressures of life." Most of the clergy take the attitude as expressed by one rector: "I always treat a self-inflicted death as the result of illness and, therefore, have no problem with offering a Christian burial." Whether this applies to the self-styled new approach of using death in a calm intellectual manner, without so-called mental confusion, is another matter—a matter that clergy will now have to deal with.

Most clergy feel that there is a "better way" of dealing with problems that lead people to self-destruction. The dilemma is how to communicate those better ways. Some admit that "it also takes a strong person to cope with the situation of living and then to go on living." One rector told me, "My best friend of twenty-one years killed himself in March 1979. The pain and turmoil may be over for him, but not for his wife, children, and friends." When this priest was asked "What are the pro's and the con's of suicide?", he answered, "For many, there is no pro to suicide." Most of the clergy whom I have asked about this subject think that the general circumstance of suicide relates to depression, lack of purpose, and weak religious life on the part of the troubled or even untroubled person. Most are willing to refer their pastoral problems for psychiatric help since they find the individual world view of the patient hopeless. What the clergy are trying to do in their fight against suicide is to give the person something to live for. One clergyman who pastors the elderly said, "I am convinced (in certain geriatric situations, for example) that the desire to die ought to be affirmed. There is a point when the Christian hope in the Resurrection needs implementation. The counselor's insight would be to remove any guilt about a desire for the end to come. Thus, the counselor facilitates the process, enabling the person to accept their condition and die a natural death in peace." There is a difference between natural death and encouraged death. A television program participant suggested that one might have people around oneself (friends) to affirm the potential suicide's belief in the right to die and to do so by encouraging one's wish with intellectual affirmation and discussion. But, after death, then what? Do those who remain have peace? Do they develop guilt as they go on in life, having aided the victim? Would their role have any effect on their own wish to join the one who committed the act? Could this effect an unconscious chain reaction? Because one person does it, must the next person do it? Like clergy, doctors stand in a strange position regarding advice on suicide. A Philadelphia physician shared this thought with me: "Even for a patient who has pain, distressing incurable illness, or just gradual mental deterioration, the problem of having sufficient mental capacity to reach out for the 'black bottle' is not always possible. It is, in such cases, that I believe euthanasia may come to be an accepted thing; although, it obviously is a very dangerous legal privilege, and certainly very careful legal factors must be taken into account. Personally, I feel that if I were faced with an incurable, painful, distressful disease, I would feel no pangs of conscience about reaching for the 'black bottle.'" Perhaps this doctor is motivated by the extent of suffering he has witnessed. Death could be only a secular problem for some physicians.

Patients commit, and are committing, suicide. In Switzerland, between 1965 and 1978, a survey revealed that five hundred seventy-four patients on maintenance renal dialysis took their own lives.[1] Doctors also commit suicide, especially physicians on probation. A study in Oregon revealed that in a group of forty doctors, eight committed suicide and two attempted suicide as a result of being on probation or being investigated. This took place in a thirteen month period. The study was done by Ralph Crawshaw, M.D., and his colleagues at the University of Oregon Health Science Center.[2]

A retired psychiatrist friend provided the most helpful insights for me, as a pastor, dealing with depressive suicidal types. As a physician and a former director of a mental health clinic, he avoided prescribing sedatives to depressed patients. He agreed that especially in cases of bereavement religious faith is of great help and that, in his experience as in my own and that of my clergy friends, it is difficult to classify suicidal cases. In his opinion, nine out of ten who talk of suicide will never make a serious attempt; but as articles and books indicate, threats should not be dismissed lightly.

The secular approach to prevent suicide should be psychiatric. Robert Clark, M.D., feels that those who speak of suicide should have an evaluation by an experienced professional. It is not a field for amateurs, however well meaning. In this sense, Dr. Clark believes that such call-in numbers with volunteers manning telephones in self-appointed agencies, however well meaning, do not do the job required. If the threat seems serious, there should be in-patient care, once or twice a week, with no waiting. If antidepressant medication is prescribed, it should be guided cautiously by the hands of a reliable relative or close friend of the patient. Medications are toxic in themselves.

Dr. Clark believes that, in psychotherapy, the

first aim is to let the patient know you are concerned. The patient should have the privilege of calling you day or night, but if the patient is of the hysterical type, the person helping out must realize that he or she will shoulder a great burden. The patient must be talked to about links to other people, relatives, and—especially in the case of teenagers—friends, clergy, and those who can be depended upon who would be saddened or hurt if he or she committed suicide. This physician's practical approach has been to talk with one important person in the patient's background to warn of the dangers, to make practical suggestions, and to give that person his telephone number. Dr. Clark sees the lonely, isolated person as the most difficult and older people as the least apt to obtain help or to tell anyone before he or she attempts death. Alcoholics and drug users are especially vulnerable. Dr. Clark is a physician who believes everything should be done to prevent suicide. "We have an obligation to help prevent suicide. We also have a concern with the problems of after suicide."

In the *Encyclopedia of Bioethics* (1978) the obligations prohibiting suicide are discussed. What are they? Obligations to other people. In killing oneself we injure the group "by depriving it of whatever contribution I could make. . . . The person who commits suicide is often someone who has been inadequately loved and cared for, who is isolated . . . and . . . [suicide] stems from a breakdown of community" (p. 1620). One is reminded of the direct words of Saint Thomas Aquinas: "Every man is of the community; hence, in killing himself he does an injury to the community."

In another area there are obligations to oneself. In this area "some policy choices leading to self-destruction may be moral, but those in which self-interest is the reason for the self-destruction cannot be" (p. 1621). As Saint Thomas Aquinas further pointed out "a prohibition on suicide is part of natural law ... self-destruction is a violation of charity to God" (p. 1621).

The religious obligations are especially important to this book. The encyclopedia reminds us that traditions of self-death can be viewed from different faiths and periods. We have mentioned this in another chapter.

Although there have already been attempts to predict suicidal types from personality types, these tests have not been very successful. If these tests were very successful and could be relied upon, it might be possible to intervene in the early years of a person's life when patterns are not yet firmly set.

Philosopher Manly Palmer Hall says: "A prime prospect for suicide is the person who refuses to accept graciously his proper place in society."[3] I agree with this in many ways. My own pastoral experience is often confined to adults and youth that cannot seem to find their way toward a meaningful contribution to life, which lifts them to a respect for themselves and a stimulation for living. Although the secular world is, by far, not the total impetus for life, I find that people who have lost their religious impulse, sense of mystery, aesthetic viewpoint, and devotional mood are prone also to misery. When these two aspects combine—the secular negative and the religious negative—the person is in danger.

If there are touching stories about suicide that fall into the category of some kind of self-sacrifice, then this is one that a friend experienced. It concerns a Latvian displaced person camp after World War II. The man who gave me this account was close to many families that came to the United States. One particular case haunted his emotions. A family was to leave the camp in Europe. All members of the family had to take and pass a tuberculosis test. Nine members of the family passed, however the grandfather failed. Therefore he could not journey to the United States. The entire family decided to remain with the the grandfather. That evening the grandfather went alone for a short walk. Shortly afterward, his dead body was found.

Anguish and guilt in the human soul can also be a horrible and exhausting experience. The following story, which took place about thirty-five years ago in New York City, is about one such tormented person. A cleaning woman came into a room in the Tudor Hotel on Forty-second Street. Upon entering the room, she found a baby who was only a few hours old. A note was left beside the baby. Apparently, the young mother of the baby had taken a room, delivered the baby herself, and then walked to the East River and drowned herself.

Edwin S. Shneidman, Ph.D., said: "Suicide is essentially something other than a thoughtful process. The person who is suicidal focuses on self-destruction and his vision is limited. He does not think beyond the act that he is about to commit."[4] One of the major reasons for this book is to encourage just that—to think beyond the act.

Should you commit suicide? No. Of course not. If you are young and in good health, whatever may be your problems, suicide is *not* the answer. Time is on your side. And time can usually be counted upon to bring healing. Almost all of the problems of young people are time-oriented; that is, there is time to change one's mind, time to explore other courses of action, time to talk, time to listen, time to reflect.

Youth has its rewards, but so does age. Memories, experiences, the knowledge of accomplishments are some of the rewards of age. But now there is also a different life-style, now there is a waiting for death. That is nature's way.

I think it is very important to remember that not a single one of the men and women of wisdom and religious and moral insight in times past believed that suicide was the proper course of action for young people, middle-aged people, or even the elderly. Unfortunately we are all the victims of a technological age in which we are both the recipients and the pawns of medicine.

As we have seen, it is entirely possible to find perfectly good arguments on either side of the case: for suicide and against suicide. But in *no* case does the argument, whether religious, psychological, or theological, apply to young men and women who are in good health as they face the future. And when I say good health I mean good physical health. (Poor psychological health is usually so closely connected to poor physical health as well as to the age that it is nearly impossible to separate the two.) To my mind this rules out drug addicts, including alcoholics, and all the other unfortunate victims of our highly technological, impersonal, and materialistic society, whose suicides are conveniently listed on the police records as caused by "temporary insanity." Many of these types are mentioned in this book. The solution to psychological problems is *not* suicide.

I do not want to be misunderstood: I stand unequivocally against suicide as a solution to the problems of anyone at any age. But, we must realize that people over the age of sixty-five are taking a different viewpoint toward suicide, and statistics, printed material, and the media are proving a new but not necessarily correct attitude. Many levels of society are taking a long, hard look at the question of suicide.

I have no quarrel with the theological doctrine (which must always rest finally on one's understanding of the nature of faith) that we are placed here on this earth for a purpose known to Divine Providence. But there are those today who are no longer sure that the God who has given us the mysteriously combined gifts of human reason and human spirit somehow willfully withdraws that gift when a mature human being, at the end of a long and fruitful life, is faced with all of the modern consequences of medical interference with death. The question is, Who is truly mature enough to reason his or her own death? Nothing will stop the "mature" person from suicide if in his or her own mind his or her reasoning is clear. Is it clear? Do we really know enough about the ancient idea of the "spiritual world," "other world," or "other side" to cope with such a decision? If we have no feeling or insight for such "other dimensions," then there is an added reason to using our supposed "maturity" to affirm our death wish as a journey to nowhere. Suicide is just as wrong for the mature person as for the immature.

Yes, our society has feared death, but mainly because we have built for ourselves a mentality that is radically disconnected from its spiritual roots. We have surrounded ourselves with both laws and customs, as well as theological and psychological doctrines, that protect us against death—against the fear of death, that is. The trouble is that such protection does not work. Nor is it helped by the fact that so many clergy do not preach about the afterlife—and for that matter disbelieve in it.

Death itself is not to be feared, contrary to the hell-fire and brimstone sermons of years gone by and even the eternal punishment belted out by what is supposed to be a loving God. But, when it comes to suicide we deal with a further mystery in the drama of death. We just don't know enough to take the risk.

The Apostle Paul was quite serious when he wrote to his friends in Corinth: "For this perishable nature must put on the imperishable, and this mortal nature must put on immortality." Then he reminded them of the older words: "Death is swallowed up in victory. O death, where is thy victory? O death, where is thy sting?" Have we heard those words so many times that they have become meaningless to us? Or are we afraid to believe them? Should they be a stimulus for suicide? Should we use them to encourage self-destruction. I doubt if they were offered with that purpose in mind. Only one of the Twelve committed suicide. Only one made death occur by his own hand. Why did not all the Apostles commit suicide? They were not taught to commit suicide.

I felt that I once came close to death. I recounted it in an earlier book *(The Spiritual Frontier)*. It was a psychic experience that took me beyond faith—and death.

One evening, while I was attending seminary, I returned to my room from visiting a college science instructor of mine who was in the hospital dying.

As I prepared for bed, my thoughts were of this brilliant and wise man to whom I owed a great intellectual debt. It was he who perhaps first showed me why life after death was perfectly credible on grounds of reason as well as of faith. He was a truly mature person. He believed one must live with nature rather than sidestep it. Perhaps that is why he did not commit suicide. He did suffer, but with dignity and a sense of the unknown. There were reason and faith in this man of science.

With heavy thoughts it was hard to sleep, but finally I dozed off.

Suddenly I was looking down at myself.

Crazy? Yes, but true. I was looking at myself on the bed below. I was watching myself sleep, my chest rhythmically rising and falling. It was uncanny, but not frightening.

Indeed, I felt exhilarated, in ecstasy. Along with my body I had shrugged off gravity. Now I was as light as a bubble. By using my will I discovered it was possible for me to move around.

In those first moments of fierce joy I was not conscious of having a body at all—not even one down below, waiting for me. Yet I felt undiminished. There was no sense that part of me was missing. This, I knew, was all of me that really mattered, somehow outside my body. *Me.*

Suddenly I saw my body as a mere container, wonderful in its way, yet still a prison into which I had been squeezed all my life. Now, for the first time, I had room to stretch.

Physical barriers were meaningless. I passed through the walls of the room as easily as a thought would and was outside in the clear winter's night, feeling no cold, for I was beyond cold and heat, rejoicing in my buoyant freedom.

The stars were more quiveringly beautiful than I had ever seen them, or was I seeing them with different eyes? But I knew, as never before, that I was more immortal than the stars.

There was, I understood, an ineffable perfect plan that contained all that was, is, and is to be—and I was part of it.

This for me, at that moment, was not an act of faith but of *knowing.*

I thought of the seminary chapel, two blocks from my room, where I prayed each day. Instantly I was there, looking down on it, relishing the sight of it and all that it meant for me.

Then, like the guilty thought of an errand undone, something pulled at me. I felt a tug, as though I were a balloon on the end of a string, like the idea of the silver cord that had not been broken.

Had it been a dream?

Never for a moment could I believe that. No, the experience was too lucid, too utterly real. There was nothing in the least dreamlike about it. As a matter of fact, by comparison, my normal waking state seemed the dream.

For those few moments I had not been asleep but, probably for the first time in my life, truly awake.

Parapsychologists call what happened to me and others in this book an out-of-the-body experience. It has happened to countless people—psychiatrists (the great Dr. Carl Jung), writers (Ernest Hemingway, Somerset Maugham), scientists (Sir Aukland Geddes) as well as farmers, bankers, and candlestick makers.

Some have been hurled out of their bodies by the shock of an accident. Some, as we have noted, have died and been medically revived. Others have doffed their physical selves during sleep, as I did, or under the influence of drugs, and others have apparently mastered the art of shedding their bodies at will.

The experience leaves everyone with personal convictions. Human personality transcends the limits of the body and, therefore, survives bodily death. Questions remain as to how we survive, and in what manner, as time moves us into eternity forever.

This was for me a luminous spiritual discovery revealed through a psychic experience.[5]

So it is that my faith and my psychic experiences alike tell me that everything has purpose. Not a tear is wasted, not a cup of water given in vain. All experience is part of some great whole. All rivers flow toward one immortal sea. All paths lead irresistibly at last to one great homecoming. But I am not so sure about the purpose of suicide and the results of suicide in a divine plan.

Although we are *never* outside the purpose of God or the love of God, we can disrupt his purpose for us on earth by suicide.

Life begins. And life ends. Death is a part of life, but in the natural order of things. Does the time of death or the condition of death or the means of death really matter? We do not know. We do know that life is not a game in which we outwit God or attempt to elude his purpose for us.

Death is not the end of everything. It is the beginning. Eternity begins now and continues, but the time is reserved for God alone.

Chapter 6

The Case Against Suicide

"A suicide opposes the purpose of his Creator, he arrives in the other world as one who has deserted his post; he must be looked upon as a rebel against God."

—IMMANUEL KANT

I want to remind my reader again that this is not a psychological textbook aimed at dealing with the "why" of suicide. I am in full agreement with Dr. Karl Menninger that suicide is a most complex event and never merely a simple action.[1] There are no simple cause-and-effect connections involved in the act of suicide—psychologically, sociologically, or theologically. Any such connections in any individual case lie buried with the suicide's body. It is unlikely that anyone will ever know all the details of the self-destruction of another. When we say "Why did he do it?" we are asking a question that not even the person himself or herself could answer. And this is especially true of people who have not had the opportunity to consider all of the aspects of suicide.

Nevertheless, I think that it is useful to review the elements that make up the solid case *against* the decision to commit suicide. To do this, let us first look at some of the stories that recount actual suicides. Consider the following list:

1. Retired Judge Peter F. Hagan plunged fourteen floors to his death from his apartment on Rittenhouse Square in Philadelphia.

2. Retired President James M. Skinner of the Philco Corporation was found dead in his car in his closed garage with the car motor running.

3. Philip L. Graham, president and chief executive officer of The Washington Post Company and of *Newsweek* magazine, shot himself.

4. James V. Forrestal, United States secretary of defense, leaped to his death.

5. James Bentley Sommerall, former board chairman of the Pepsi-Cola Company, shot himself.

6. Eli M. Black, chairman of the billion dollar United Brands conglomerate, jumped to his death from the forty-fourth floor of the Pan-Am Building in New York City.

7. William F. Knowland, U.S. senator and Republican majority leader in the 1950s and a California newspaper publisher, shot himself.

8. U.S. Attorney Robert Morse jumped five floors to his death in New York City. He was chief federal prosecutor for the Eastern District of New York.

9. Ethel duPont Warren, former wife of Franklin

D. Roosevelt, Jr., and heiress to the duPont fortune, hanged herself in her bathroom.

10. Vernon C. Walston, president of Walston & Company, one of the nation's largest and most respected brokerage firms, killed himself with a shotgun.

I compiled this list from the files of my local newspaper. And the list goes on and on. There is no end to it, because it keeps growing every day. As the reader has already noted, I have listed only a few prominent men and women whose names and careers make up a cross section of "successful" people in our society. I have not even begun to list the nearly thirty thousand people from all ranks of life who commit suicide in the United States *each year.* In the United Kingdom about 100 males and 60 females per million persons commit suicide. Even though the British have the lowest suicide rate in Europe, a group in England called The Samaritans, founded by an Anglican vicar named Chad Varah, received 250,000 calls in one year from people contemplating suicide. They were also aware of a dramatic increase in suicides in the Spring.

I will have something to say in a later chapter about the enormous number of suicides among the young, but at this point, a single example of that aspect of the problem is appropriate: Mrs. Mary Connelly is the mother of seven children. Their IQs range from 130 to 150, thus putting them in the genius or near-genius class. Five of those seven children have contemplated suicide at one time or another, she said. So she has had firsthand experience with what many experts have called one of the most serious wastes of this country's most precious natural resources—its gifted children.[2]

The case against suicide seems so self-evident. In our society the subject is so much a taboo, however, that we do not really see why anyone should even raise the question. But the brutal facts are with us every day. Even as I write, a man walked into my study to tell me that his fifteen-year-old son had just attempted suicide. And in the course of our conversation it was apparent that neither the man nor his wife had ever given an instant's thought to the possibility that their own son might destroy himself. It was almost as if their lifelong attitude had been "this is the kind of thing that happens to other people—never to us."

I am sure that Dr. Karl Menninger has summarized the general attitude toward suicide. In the Foreword to his book *Essays in Self-Destruction* he says: "How can we get people to realize that suicide is only a dramatic, individual example of human self-destructiveness and that we can and must combat it?"[3] That is, we seem to have a foregone conclusion that everyone everywhere is automatically against suicide. Yet there are more than thirty thousand people every year who prove us wrong! How can we get people to realize that the case against suicide is not really closed so long as we persist in not looking at the problem directly?

When the Public Broadcasting Service (PBS) offered its television stations a documentary program made up of the videotaped nineteen hours of interviews held by Jo Roman before she committed suicide, the newspaper reports on the Associated Press wire said:

> Public television stations in three states are refusing to broadcast a documentary on the suicide of a New York artist. The stations say the program is a potentially dangerous, one-sided advocacy of suicide. "We have a great fear of someone calling us to say, 'My mother committed suicide after watching your program,' " said Midge Ramsey of Connecticut Public Broadcasting.

But the implication of the refusal to broadcast the program is that if we don't talk about the subject of suicide, maybe it will go away. That is, so long as people think that the case *against* suicide is self-validating, self-evident, and closed—then, of course, no one will do it. Not true. Tragically, not true.

All of the successful people whose names appear in the long list given above did the wrong thing. Had they given themselves more time to think through their problems, had their cry for help been heard, had they been able to dig themselves out of their depression, perhaps they would have seen the error of their ways and suicide would not have been their way out. But no one had convinced them that suicide is the wrong decision and the wrong action.

Dr. Louis Wekstein, in his book *Handbook of Suicidology: Principles, Problems and Practice,* has two sentences in the Introduction that surely represent the consensus of contemporary Western thinking about suicide:

Life is precious above all else, and once rooted there is a tenacious attempt to hold on to it and to maintain it at all costs. This clinging to life in the face of tragedy, adversity, torture, anguish, humiliation, the ravages of old age—even interminable pain when death is manifestly imminent—is characteristic of the overwhelming majority of humanity.[4]

Since the time of St. Augustine (A.D. 395) the Church has been adamantly against suicide and has proscribed it for all members. Following the lead of the Church, all of the European states passed laws against suicide. Moreover, since Freud's work on the subject, suicidology has found its proper niche within the field of psychopathology. That is, the consensus among psychologists and psychopathologists is that the act of suicide is evidence of a mind under serious tension, if not true derangement. In fact, the recent dramatic rise in the number of crisis intervention centers is ample evidence of the new role that lay people themselves are assuming under the guidance of professional psychiatrists and psychologists. The most famous, and probably the most successful, of these suicide prevention groups is The Samaritans. This group of lay people was organized by Chad Varah, an Anglican priest, in London in 1966. The success of this British organization in preventing suicide has encouraged the establishment of similar groups in the United States.

When we speak of the case against suicide as being so self-evident that ordinary people in the ordinary circumstances of life never even think about it, it is well to look at the words of Dr. Wekstein (whose book is, incidentally, one of the best on the subject). He makes the unequivocal statement that "the suicidal crisis represents an event with lethal urgency, and no efforts can be spared for scholastic deliberation and judgmental attitudes."[5] It is precisely because of the element of "lethal urgency" involved in every suicide that all of us must *know* what we think about suicide. Only then can we act to prevent it. In my view, suicide is always and everywhere to be prevented.

The very influential Public Affairs Committee, a "non-profit educational organization founded in 1935 to develop new educational techniques for the American public on vital economic and social problems and to issue concise and interesting pamphlets dealing with such problems," has a pamphlet called *Dealing With The Crisis of Suicide.* In it, the authors, Calvin J. Frederick and Louise Lague, say, "Suicide is the denial of a human being's most urgent need—self-preservation—and it contradicts the valuation of human life that is implicit in democratic and social ethics." Again, this is the case against suicide in its simplest form. These same authors go on to make a cogent appeal:

> The 30,000 suicides in the United States each year cost the states and municipalities an estimated four billion dollars. This includes primarily such expenses as emergency facilities, brief hospitalization, and loss of income.
>
> But no amount of money can compensate for the shame a family is made to feel. A suicide in the family is still a stigma that may be a burden for years to come. Aside from religious and cultural

taboos, people may assume that the family must have been responsible in some way for a person's reaching such a point of desperation... There is the fear that the community blames the family for the suicide, or attributes to them the emotional instability associated with suicide. And, finally, there are the very real feelings of guilt. Were they, in fact, insensitive to Dad's worries? Did they, in effect, murder him?

The survivors themselves may suffer serious emotional and mental crises that could result in their becoming victims of suicide too.[6]

This pamphlet comes to the conclusion that is generally recognized to be the universally understood answer to the problem. In one sentence it sums up that consensus: "Suicide need no longer be a major cause of death in our country because it can be prevented. We know, too, that we should not let people kill themselves even if they say they want to. The gift of life is too important, and the widening ring of tragedy a suicide leaves behind is too devastating."

Thus, it is generally held that suicide is bad for everyone concerned—no matter what the circumstances or conditions of life. That dictum applies to all categories of society—rich man, poor man, beggar man, thief.

But recently the situation has become somewhat more complicated by the attention that medical doctors are drawing to their profession and to themselves. This is, indeed, a matter of serious concern for all of society. Here is the most succinct statement of the problem that I have seen at the time of this writing. On May 12, 1980, the Associated Press news wire distributed this article to its subscribers across the country:

> A national program should be established to study the incidences and reasons for suicides among physicians, an article in the *Journal of the American Medical Association* says.
>
> The need for the study was one conclusion reached by a team of medical, psychiatric, and sociological professionals who investigated the suicides of eight physicians in Oregon.
>
> The eight physicians were among about 40 on probation or under investigation for probation by the Oregon Board of Medical Examiners in the Spring of 1977. The suicides occurred during a 13 month period prior to that time. Two other physicians in that group also had attempted suicide.
>
> The suicide rate for the general population is about 15 per 100,000. Among physicians it is thought to be about 77 per 100,000, says the Journal article.[7]

The case against suicide becomes particularly strong when it involves the men and women who are themselves charged with the health and well-being of society at large.

A study completed some years ago, but one that could be duplicated by similar research in any of our larger cities, is based on these statistics: In the six-year period from January 1, 1934, to January 1, 1940, ninety-three New York City policemen committed suicide.

In his essay on this situation Dr. Paul Friedman says: "The suicide rate among policemen had reached alarming proportions at that time, and what particularly triggered public interest was the suicide of a police inspector who had been on the force for thirty years."[8]

There is some evidence that there is a continuing incidence of suicide among policemen in all major cities.[9] But, again, we are faced with a "case against suicide" when we realize that policemen, as well as medical doctors, are society's means of protecting itself. It makes a very strong case, indeed.

To my knowledge there are no accurate statistics on the number of suicides among clergymen, social workers, nurses, and others in the helping professions. But it is generally recognized that the number is greater than usually expected—and growing. And to add these people to the case against suicide makes that case even stronger. We simply cannot afford to waste such people!

Let me close this chapter with the story of a man who might have been expected to commit suicide. He did not. He was morally convinced that suicide is wrong.

The man was the father-in-law of a close friend of mine. Both my friend and his father-in-law are Presbyterian ministers. I shall use pseudonyms throughout their story.

The Reverend Mr. Jones was age ninety-two when he died. He had been a clergyman for over sixty years, on the foreign mission field and as a parish minister. All of his life he had exemplified what is sometimes called "a gentleman of the old school." He was self-disciplined. He was meticulous in dress and habits. He was gracious and kind to all he knew. His people loved him, and he returned that love in many different ways. He was, in every respect, what his people called him: "A man of God."

At age eighty-nine Mr. Jones suffered a stroke. Concurrently, it was discovered that he had developed prostate cancer. And he began to display the signs of advancing senility.

His doctor admitted him to the hospital for an operation intended to relieve the cancer to whatever extent was possible. Because his stroke had left him unable to communicate clearly and because his mind was no longer able to function consistently, he was restrained by straps to his bed.

After the operation, near midnight one night, he tried to get out of bed. Somehow he was able to untie the straps and get to the foot of his bed. There he pitched over the railing. In the fall, he tore loose the stitches, struck his head badly, and twisted an arm almost behind his back.

The operation had to be done all over again—on an emergency basis, by an emergency room surgeon on duty that night.

For the next *three years,* Mr. Jones endured agony of both mind and body. He was no longer able to dress himself, feed himself, or manage the normal bodily functions. Every decision had to be made for him by someone else.

But he hung on. Occasionally, his mind cleared, and he was able to recognize who he was, where he was, and the condition he was in. During one such instance his son-in-law, my friend, thinking it would be helpful, asked him this question: "Dad, it may be that the end is near. How do you feel about that?"

The old gentleman shook his head feebly and tried to smile. "I'm ready," he whispered. "But I don't want to go before my time. I'm tired out with the pain and the embarrassment. I wish I could go right now. But it's God's will for me to stay awhile longer, I guess."

After it was over, some weeks later, my friend said to me, "Did I do the right thing for him? Should I have helped him to die—months ago? If he had really been able to see himself in that condition, wouldn't he have wanted someone to help him get on with it?"

He shook his head, thought a minute, and then answered his own questions.

"No. He was straight out of the old Judeo-Christian tradition. He built his life on the Genesis teaching—God created life and saw that it was good. He was committed all the way to the end to the idea that his life was God's—and that only God knew the time and place of his death."

The case against death is a strong one. It is built into all of us, especially those of us who are in the ancient tradition of the Jews and Christians—whether we are practicing believers or not.

Suicide is *not* the answer.

Chapter 7

The Philosophers and Theologians

―――――――――

"Disregarding the demands made by religion, one might well ask: Why should it be more laudable for an old man who senses the decline of his powers to await his slow exhaustion and dissolution than in full consciousness to set himself a limit? Suicide is in this case a wholly natural obvious action, which as a victory for reason ought fairly to awaken reverence: and did awaken it in those ages when the heads of Greek philosophy and the most upright Roman patriots were accustomed to die by suicide."

—NIETZSCHE

Nietzsche is not one of my most-admired philosophers. Yet his question and his reference to the history of the idea of suicide do remind us again that the act of self-destruction, however epidemic it may be in our own day, has a long history behind it. This is not a brand-new problem appearing out of the blue for Americans and certainly not for Europeans. Denmark, for example, has the highest suicide rate in the Western world followed by Finland and Sweden. The problem is universal. It varies only by statistics.

The literary critic A. Alvarez is certain that "suicide has permeated Western culture like a dye that cannot be washed out."[1] And he also believes that half of the literature of the world is about death. I have already said something about the fascination that death has for many people, but James Hillman puts it most starkly when he says: "We never come fully to grips with life until we are willing to wrestle with death. If we want to move toward self knowledge and the experience of reality, then an enquiry into suicide becomes the first step."[2]

It is true, I think, that we are at the point in our civilization where we are both willing and able to ask ourselves some questions about death that could not have been asked in, for example, the Middle Ages, or even in the early years of the twentieth century. These may be, to be sure, the basic questions that the professional philosophers and theologians have been dealing with for many years. But today in the unearthly light of the possibility of nuclear war, we are all asking philosophical questions that lead to theological answers. So it is well to take a moment to look back over history to try to find out how we got where we are. The exercise may sound dull and uninspiring, but it was proved long ago that we ignore history to our own peril. And, anyway, as I said earlier, death is a tantalizing mystery to most of us!

In the period of the Renaissance, Montaigne was looking at the question of legal suicide. By that time, such suicide had become almost a custom for those whose lives had lost purpose and meaning. He puts it this way:

Death is a remedy against all evils: It is a most assured haven, never to be feared, and often to be sought: All comes to one period, whether man make an end of himself, or whether he endure it; whether he run before his day, or whether he expect it: whence soever it come, it is ever his owne, where ever the thread be broken, it is all there, it's the end of the web. The voluntariest death is the fairest. Life dependeth on the will of others, death on ours.[3]

The idea that "death is never to be feared" was not invented by Montaigne. It had come down to him through the tradition of Western civilization. Indeed, it had been a part of the early Christian tradition, as we have seen. But it was most likely Montaigne who first ignored the authority of the Church on the subject and based his comments on the classical philosophers such as Seneca. Following Seneca's lead, Montaigne treats death as if it were a natural part of life. The Roman custom of suicide is to him a noble and natural act.

Two hundred years later, David Hume in Scotland found no valid moral, legal, or religious arguments against suicide. He concluded that suicide may, indeed, even be useful not only for the individual but also for society. In combating the theory that suicide was a crime against God, Hume wrote:

Do you imagine that I repine at Providence, or curse my creation, because I go out of life, and put a period to a being which, were it to continue, would render me miserable? Far be such sentiments from me. I am only convinced of a matter of fact which you yourself acknowledge possible, that human life may be unhappy; and that my existence, if further prolonged, would become ineligible: but I thank Providence, both for the good which I have already enjoyed, and for the power with which I am endowed of escaping the ills that threaten me. To you it belongs to repine at Providence, who foolishly imagine that you have no such power; and who must still prolong a hated life, though loaded with pain and sickness, with shame and poverty. When I fall upon my own sword, therefore, I receive my death equally from the hands of the Diety as if it had proceeded from a lion, a precipice, or a fever.[4]

Hume went on to say that, in his opinion, nothing happens anywhere in the universe without the "Consent and Cooperation of Providence." That being the case, he concludes: "Neither does my death, however voluntary, happen without the consent of Providence; and whenever pain or sorrow so far overcome my patience as to make me tired of life, I may conclude that I am recalled from my station in the clearest and most express terms. . . . It is a kind of blasphemy to imagine that any created being can disturb the order of the world or invade the business of Providence."

As for the effect on society of his suicide, Hume said: "A man who retires from life does no harm to society, he only ceases to do good; which, if it is an injury, is of the lowest kind."

David Hume has been called a social utilitarian. Had he lived in this country and at a later age, he would probably have been called an American pragmatist. At any rate, his concern for society is seen most strongly in his statement that "suicide is the only way that we can be useful to society, by setting an example, which, if imitated, would preserve to every one his chance to happiness in life, and would effectually free him from all danger or misery."

Still later, as philosophy gave way in both England and America to the new "social sciences," it became clear that suicide was to be treated in a social rather than an individual context. However much it may seem an individual act to the one who contemplates suicide, it is the effect on society that has been weighed and measured and theorized about.

In 1897 Emile Durkheim, the French founder of sociology, published what has since become the classic in its field. His book *Suicide,* using the statistical method, was not concerned with any moral or criminal aspects of the matter; he treated suicide simply as a fact of society. In his view, all suicides could be classified under three categories: the egoistic (usually the loner or the romantic), the altruistic (in which suicide is a sacrifice for a cause), and the anomic (in which the individual is disoriented so much that he cannot make the necessary adjustments to his life-situation).

In my role as a religious counselor, I have often

observed that sociological and psychological theories come and go. People who sit in my study asking for help simply cannot cope with intricate theories. So it seems to me that my best service to such individuals is to help them determine whether or not they are able to deal with their life-situations realistically. And since they have come to me, rather than to a psychologist, I assume that they are asking for help within the Christian context of faith.

In the Jewish tradition, suicide has always been regarded as a crime against God. To be sure, the five cases of suicide recounted in the Old Testament are said to be unusual because of the circumstances under which they occurred. During the Maccabean period of Jewish history, there is a story of the mother who deliberately flung herself into a fire after having watched her seven sons killed by the tyrant (IV Macc. 17:1). There is also the account of Razis, who killed himself in order to avoid torture at the hands of his captors (II Macc. 14:42).

By the time of Josephus, the most famous Jewish historian, a suicide was held to give up his share in the world to come. Hence, he was not given full honors at the time of burial. In fact, the law as stated in the Talmud stipulated that no suicide was to receive any kind of eulogy or public mourning. That law was later amended by way of defining a suicide as applying only to an individual who had announced in advance the method by which he intended to kill himself. It also decreed that no child could be regarded as a deliberate suicide (*Semahoth* 1:15).

The position had begun to change by the time of the medieval period. At that time, authorities held that a suicide who did away with himself under severe mental or physical strain, or while insane, was not to be regarded as a sinner (*Midrash Gen.* 65:22). Thus, in the account by Josephus of the entire garrison at Masada committing suicide rather than surrendering to the Romans, there is no condemnation of this action as suicide.[5]

As is well-known, during World War II in the concentration camps many Jews or their relatives bribed the guards so as to permit them to commit suicide in order to avoid further torture.

In the Roman Catholic tradition, suicide means an unlawful moral act, either positive or negative, by which one directly causes his own death. That is, it is possible for an individual to commit suicide by a positive act of self-destruction or by the neglect of something that he knows to be necessary for his continued life. In the Roman Catholic view, a man who bleeds to death because he will not close an open artery is no less a suicide than a man who opens an artery in order to take his life.

A moral distinction is made between direct and indirect suicide. Direct suicide is committed when one intends to cause his own death *as a thing desired for its own sake* (as when death is preferred to the meaninglessness of life), or as a means to an end (as when one hangs himself to avoid prosecution or to provide his heirs with the proceeds of insurance).

"Suicide is indirect when death itself is not desired, either as a means or as an end, but when it is simply seen as a likely consequence of an act the immediate effect and purpose of which is something other than death (as when a man turns his car out of the way and over a precipice to avoid a collision with an oncoming school bus.)"[6]

Generally speaking, Roman Catholic theologians have, since the time of Augustine, regarded direct suicide as a violation of the commandment "Thou shalt not kill" (Ex. 20:13). That is, the command has been understood to forbid the taking of human life, no matter whose. Saint Thomas Aquinas held that suicide is "contrary to the inclination implanted by the Creator in every creature to conserve itself in existence and to resist forces which would destroy it." This was considered to be a matter of natural law contained in the revealed law of God.

Aquinas also taught that suicide is an offense against society since, in taking his own life, man deprives the community of something that rightfully belongs to it. Finally, he held that life is a gift from God given to be used and enjoyed—but in submission to God who continues to hold power over life and death. The inference, then, is that suicide is a sin against God.

Roman Catholic theologians are agreed that suicide is intrinsically evil and that there can be no circumstances that justify it. In the case of indirect suicide, the individual is said to have committed an unlawful act since he is not only forbidden to take his own life, he is also forbidden to expose it to "unreasonable risk." Even so, there are cases that may be justified, but the greater the risk to life, the greater must be the compensating good in order to make the justification possible.

People who actually commit suicide are not to be given ecclesiastical burials *unless* they have shown some signs of repentance before their death. However, if it is doubtful whether a person who committed suicide was responsible for his or her act (was mentally deranged), the doubt is decided in his or her favor—provided that no scandal is likely to ensue.[7]

The Protestant position on suicide is pluralistic, as might be expected. To the fundamentalist Protestant, suicide is a crime against God and will most certainly be harshly judged. David Wilkerson is probably the most prominent spokesman of this view:

> People who commit suicide do not just die and then decay into nothingness. Death is not the end at all: it is just the beginning. Every suicide victim goes straight to the judgment hall of Christ, to answer to Him for rejecting His priceless gift of life. No one can play God by taking his life. No one will ever be permitted to throw that life back into God's face. No one will be permitted to abort God's plan for his life. No one will be allowed to go into eternity with his life's work undone, without being judged as a thief.[8]

Wilkerson's book *Suicide: A Killer Is Stalking The Land!* goes on to list the "seven deadly sins" committed by one who takes his or her own life. The list begins with the statement "here is exactly what the Bible says about suicide":

1. Suicide is a form of atheism.
2. Suicide is satanic seduction.

3. Suicide is the sin of hypocrisy.
4. Suicide is the sin of pride.
5. Suicide is the sin of lying.
6. Suicide is an attack on the body of Christ.
7. Suicide is blasphemy against the Holy Ghost.[9]

I do not propose to enter into a discussion here of how Mr. Wilkerson is so sure that this list is "exactly" what the Bible says about suicide. I am more than a little appalled at his notion of "God's simple solution." Nevertheless, Wilkerson's position is certainly representative of American fundamentalistic theologians today. In 1961, the fundamentalist American Council of Churches passed a resolution that stated: "Death by suicide ends all opportunity for repentance. Almighty God created life. It is His. Murder, including self-murder, is a transgression of His law."[10]

But the theologians of the main-line Protestant traditions have not held so harsh a view. The theologians of our century who have exercised the most influence on the American Church have been almost unanimous in speaking of suicide as a sin against God. This would also be true of the British church. And I would add my own voice to theirs at that point.

But they have gone on immediately to stress the forgiveness of God for all sins, including that of suicide. Karl Barth, Dietrich Bonhoeffer, Helmut Thielicke, Reinhold Niebuhr, William Temple, John Bennett—the list goes on and on—have all insisted that although suicide is a serious matter, it is never to be considered "the unpardonable sin."

To see how far we have come, it is only necessary

to recall that in 1790 John Wesley, the great Methodist reformer, proposed that the naked bodies of female suicides be dragged through the streets. Blackstone, the revered English legal authority, wrote that for a suicide, burial was to be "in the highway, with a stake driven through the body," as though there were no difference between a suicide and a vampire. The place of burial was usually a highway crossroads (also the place of the public execution of condemned criminals), and a stone was put over the face of the suicide. Stake and stone prevented the ghost of the suicide from rising to haunt the living. My point here is that there is no record that the Church protested equating suicide with crime. (Nor did the Church protest the degradation of the suicide's body.)

Interestingly enough, the position of liberal Christianity, both clergy and laity, has not been better stated than by Arthur Schopenhauer. Although he was against suicide, in the early 1800s he wrote:

> I am of the opinion that the clergy should once and for all be challenged to give an account with what right they, without being able to show any Biblical authority, or any valid philosophical arguments, stigmatize in the pulpit and in their writings an action committed by many . . . and refuse those who voluntarily leave this world an honorable burial.[11]

The humanist (non-Christian, but nonatheist) position is depicted by such writers as Herbert A. Tonne and Thomas Szasz.

Tonne believes that the right to make a decision for oneself is a fundamental right. He says:

> If a person wishes to continue to the bitter end, that should be his right. At the same time, isn't it equally right to call it quits and to avoid the suffering and degradation that is so often a prelude to death? As it does in our other attitudes, custom influences us in our views of suicide. Someday we may praise people who meet death on their own terms—at the time, place, and manner they choose.[12]

Dr. Szasz states his own convictions even more forcefully:

> It has always boiled down to a basic question: Who owns your body? Jewish fundamentalism said God owns everything and Christianity picked up this idea and elaborated it. But since the 17th century, with the rise of science, doctors have been saying, "Take the power over the body away from God and give it to me." So—who has ownership, the person himself or the doctors?[13]

I would like to close this chapter by listing a few questions that seem to recur time and again in the public discussion of the idea of rational suicide. By this time, my reader should be well aware of how I myself would answer such questions. Nevertheless, the list of these questions will serve to crystallize for the reader the position that seems to be more and more acceptable to Americans and their British cousins these days.

1. Why is it always bad news when a doctor tells a patient and his family of terminal illness?

2. Why must we help people to live until they die their natural deaths?

3. Is it really true that the suicidal person wants desperately to live—he or she is begging to be saved?

4. Is it really true that suicide always involves tortured and tunneled logic?

5. Is life always and under all conditions better than death?

In one form or another, these are the questions that clergy, psychiatrists, social workers, and medical people are encountering today. Are they an indication of a major shift in traditional attitudes toward death?

Chapter 8

The Case Against Rational Suicide

"Intellect distinguishes between the possible and the impossible; reason distinguishes between the sensible and the senseless; even the possible can be senseless."

—MAX BORN

On October 19, 1977, the Religious News Service sent the following story to its subscribers, originating from Swarthmore, Pennsylvania. The first line read: "Morgan Sibbett, a 65-year old engineer here, said that he had allowed a longtime friend who was dying of Parkinson's disease to commit suicide in his home."

The account continued: "Dr. Wallace Proctor, 75, a dermatologist from Pocatella, Idaho, died August 16th in Mr. Sibbett's home of a drug overdose."

In further explaining the reasons for Dr. Proctor's suicide, the report said that the suicide had been planned in 1974 after Dr. Proctor had been forced to retire because of the disease. He decided to die in Pennsylvania rather than at his home in Idaho because suicide is not a crime in Pennsylvania. (This is a reflection of the Quaker influence on Pennsylvania law.) He had been suffering for some time from advanced Parkinson's disease and had discovered that he required ever-increasing doses of the medicines that were prescribed to control the trembling of his hands.

In a note to his family and friends, Dr. Proctor said: "Some of you may look upon suicide with uneasiness or disfavor, but it may also represent a logical, considerate and effective means to satisfy one's responsibility to the world."

And his friend Mr. Sibbett said, "Our leave-taking was quite matter-of-fact. They were just days of quiet reminiscence." The two friends decided to have five days together during which they went for walks, dined out, spoke of the things on their minds—and prepared for Dr. Proctor's death. Mr. Sibbett said that they shared a final dinner and reflected upon the brilliant sunset that evening. His friend then went upstairs to die.

I am retelling this story because, if I am to present properly the case against rational suicide, the reader must be quite sure of what rational suicide is. It is this idea that is so rapidly coming to the fore in the United States and Great Britain. I believe that it is quite mistaken, quite wrong. And quite unchristian. Indeed, quite against the basic truth of most of the major religious traditions of mankind.

There are two other stories that need to be reviewed in order for the reader to understand the major point that I wish to make in the case against rational suicide. I shall present these other two stories and then demonstrate what I think is the missing factor in all three instances.

Newsweek magazine, in its July 2, 1979, issue, carried an article entitled "Rational Suicide?" That story raised the issue in very clear-cut terms, and a great many people began to discuss the problem. I suspect that the idea of rational suicide had at last come out of the closet.

The story begins this way: "For 15 months artist Jo Roman planned her suicide. She completed her 250-page book espousing the right to die. She had a cameraman videotape 19 hours of a conversation on the subject with her family and friends."

Jo Roman then wrote a letter to sixty of her friends. She composed her own obituary and sent it to *The New York Times.* Early on the morning of Sunday, June 10, 1979, at age sixty-two, she said good-bye to her husband, to her daughter, and to a friend of the family. Then she took thirty-five sleeping pills, washed down with champagne.

In reflecting upon Jo Roman's suicide the writer of the *Newsweek* story pointed out that "this extraordinary suicide stemmed from her belief that people should determine their own time of death." It appears that she had earlier chosen the date of her seventy-fifth birthday, which would have been in 1992. But when told that she had contracted breast cancer, she moved the date up. The *Newsweek* writer was interested to discover that her case differed from many of those people who kill themselves because of fatal illness. Jo Roman's case was not yet critical. (In fact, the medical examiner testified that there was no evidence that the cancer had spread beyond the lymph nodes to any vital organ.) There was another difference: Jo Roman made an effort to publicize her belief that she should "create on my own terms the final stroke of my life's canvas."

In her farewell letter to her friends, she said: "I concluded that suicide need not be pathological, that rational suicide makes possible a truly ideal closing of one's life span."

When in March of 1978 she found that the disease had already spread to the lymph nodes and that, with chemotherapy, she might have two years to live, she wrote: "I knew from the outset that I would not subject myself nor those around me to the emotional strains and the physical ravages of terminal cancer. Instead, I would make the best possible calculation of a time frame within which I might count reasonably on being able to function to my satisfaction."

Around five-thirty in the morning, Jo Roman took the pills. Her friend Timmy said, "The morning was a special time for her. It meant a new life, a new day."

The other story that illustrates the idea as well as the action that is being called rational suicide comes from Great Britain.

In his book, *Jean's Way,* Derek Humphry tells of his wife's decision to end her life. When the doctors told them that she had less than a year to live because of the rapid spread of bone cancer, Jean Humphry said to her husband:

Derek, I simply don't want to go on living like this. I want you to do something for me so that if I decide I want to die I can do it on my own terms and exactly when I choose. I want you to promise me that when I ask you if this is the right time to kill myself, you will give me an honest answer one way or another and we must both understand that I'll do it at that very moment. You won't question my right and you will give me the means to do it.

The day soon came when the doctor reported to Derek Humphry that he could no longer relieve Jean's pain and that "she is worn out from fighting." Immediately, Derek Humphry made arrangements to take her home.

He tells the rest of the story in these words:

The next day was Good Friday and we spent it quietly, holding one another, listening to our stereo and occasionally reading. It was to be our last full day together. That evening I sat beside Jean's bed and tried to keep a hold on my emotions until she fell into a drugged sleep.

Next morning, Jean said, "My neck is very bad. I can't move it."

I prepared her usual dosage of medicine and pain-killing drugs which she swallowed in a gulp.

I knew that the end was here and I could not fail her.

I recalled her words, "When I die, I want to be at home with you, Derek. Whatever you do, don't let me die in the hospital." My eyes filled with tears. Then, trying to appear normal, I prepared breakfast and carried the tray into the sickroom.

"Derek?" Jean called softly.

"Yes, darling?"

"Is this the day?"

I panicked. It was the most awful day of my life. However, I had to answer, "Yes, my darling, it is."

I explained to Jean about the drugs I had gotten in preparation for this day. After a long silence, she said, "I shall die at one o'clock."

Despite my sorrow, I exalted in Jean's courage in carrying out her chosen way of death. After more than two years of suffering she was, I felt, entitled to leave this life with style and on her own terms.

It was ten minutes before one.

I dried my tears and went to get the brew of sleeping pills and pain-killers. I made two cups of strong coffee and into one I poured the potion. Then I carried them into the sickroom and placed Jean's on the table beside her.

"Is that it?" she asked.

I did not need to reply. I took her in my arms and kissed her.

"Good-bye, my love."

"Good-bye, darling."

She lifted the mug and gulped the contents down swiftly. Within seconds, she appeared to fall asleep and soon her breathing was slow and heavy.

At 1:50 P.M., on March 29, 1975, as I sat watching, she died peacefully.[1]

These three stories about Dr. Proctor, Jo Roman, and Jean Humphry illustrate a new way that people deal with death. Somehow, we think that we are "modern" when we talk about rational suicide. Not so.

Seneca the Younger (4 B.C.–A.D. 65), the Roman philosopher, statesman, and playwright, in his *Moral Letters,* says:

You may consider that life has carried some men with the greatest rapidity to the harbour, the harbour they were bound to reach even if they tarried on the way, while others it has fretted and harassed. To such a life, as you are aware, one should not always cling. For mere living is not a good, but living well. Accordingly, the wise man will live as long as he ought, not as long as he can. He will mark in what place, with whom and how he is to conduct his existence, and what he is about to do. He always reflects concerning the quality, and not the quantity, of his life. As soon as there are many events in his life that give him trouble and disturb his peace of mind, he sets himself free. And this privilege is his, not only when the crisis is upon him, but as soon as Fortune seems to be playing him false; then he looks carefully about and sees whether he ought, or ought not, to end his life on that account. He holds that it makes no difference to him whether his taking-off be natural or self-inflicted, whether it comes sooner or later. He does not regard it with fear, as if it were a great loss; for no man can lose very much when but a driblet remains. It is not a question of dying earlier or later, but of dying well or ill. And dying well means escape from the danger of dying ill.[2]

Seneca was the teacher of the most vicious of the Roman emperors, Nero. It was Nero whose actions caused Seneca to commit rational suicide. Interestingly, it has been said that in his broad moral attitudes, Seneca most resembles the Apostle Paul, who was his contemporary.

So, it is easy enough to compile a list of the distinguished men of the ancient world who committed suicide. In his book *The Savage God,* A. Alvarez mentions these: Socrates, Codrus, Charondas, Lycurgus, Cleombrotus, Cato, Zeno, Cleanthes, Seneca, and Paulina. He goes on to list other notables:

> Among many others were the Greek orators Isocrates and Demosthenes; the Roman poets Lucretius, Lucan and Labienus, the dramatist Terence, the critic Aristarchus, and Petronius Arbiter, who was the most fastidious of them all; Hannibal, Boadicea, Brutus, Cassius, Mark Antony and Cleopatra, Cocceius Nerva, Statius, Nero, Otho, King Ptolemy of Cyprus, and King Sardanapalus of Persia.[3]

Alvarez concludes that the Romans viewed suicide "with neither fear nor revulsion, but as a carefully considered and chosen validation of the way they had lived and the principles they had lived by. To live nobly also meant to die nobly and at the right moment. Everything depended upon the dominant will and a rational choice."[4]

Rational suicide does not, then, appear to be a modern idea at all. Perhaps Seneca and his colleagues did not have videotape machines by which to spread the word of their impending death by self-destruction, but nevertheless, the message has come down to us today.

We must, of course, give Dr. Proctor, Jo Roman, and Jean Humphry the benefit of the doubt and assume that each was honest, sincere, and thoughtful in making the decision that was made.

My point is that I think each made the wrong decision—a decision made for the wrong reasons, however honest and sincere.

Let me point out that these three stories exhibit differing viewpoints that deserve consideration. Dr. Proctor thought it best not to let his wife know what he proposed to do—or when. He depended upon a close friend. Jo Roman not only wanted close friends to know of her decision and her act, she also wanted the widest possible publicity for her suicide. True, she believed that this was not from any sense of vanity or self-importance, but because she truly believed that other people should recognize the reasonableness of her action in the circumstances. Jean Humphry prized most the close and intimate relationship with her husband; she wanted to make sure that their last moments together epitomized the happiness of their marriage.

It seems to me that each of these three people was asking the question raised by Seneca two thousand years ago: Since I am to die sooner or later, why not die while I am in full possession of my mind and, as much as possible, of my health? That is, they are saying that the *method* or the *means* of death is not nearly so important as the safeguarding of the relationships they cherished and the principles they lived by.

The ancient Greeks and Romans and all other pre-Christians might be expected to miss the main point of my case *against* rational suicide—although I might even argue that point at another time and place. But Dr. Proctor, Jo Roman, and Jean Humphry need not have missed it. Whether they missed the point deliberately or not is beyond our knowing now, of course.

The idea of rational suicide in our day is basically flawed and, from my understanding of the Christian faith, it is dead wrong *because* it either ignores or willfully disregards the doctrine of the compassionate suffering of Jesus Christ on the Cross.

In all of these stories of suicide of men and women, both ancient and contemporary, the outstanding element is a focus on *self*. To be sure, in some instances, perhaps all of them, there is concern about family and friends. We have already discussed the idea of community as it relates to the suicides of Dr. Van Dusen and his wife. But however much that concept is pressed, it cannot be denied that the *primary* interest of persons who commit suicide is for themselves. They believe that either they are escaping an unsatisfactory condition of life (which they themselves determine, as witness the constant repetition of the phrase "death at a time and place of my own choosing") or they are in sole command of their destiny and, therefore, have a *right* to be self-centered in this way.

In the long history of the Christian faith, the golden thread that ties it all together is the radical emphasis on the nature and purpose of suffering. And by both inference and direct teaching this new understanding of suffering is based on suffering *for others*. In the New Testament, Jesus walks as "a Man of Sorrows, acquainted with grief and suffering." Here is compassionate suffering, suffering *for others*. Nowhere in the story of Jesus' life is there any evidence that he thought of himself, of his own needs and desires, *first.* (The theologians of our day have taken to calling him "The Man for Others.")

Theologically, the most pervasive of all sins is that of selfishness. The early church fathers had a fine old Latin phrase for it: *incurvatus in se,* curving in upon oneself. *It is this constant curving in upon oneself that characterizes every single instance of suicide that I know about.* The one who commits suicide *always* thinks first of himself. The one who commits suicide *always* ignores the lesson of the compassionate suffering of Jesus Christ upon the Cross. Suffering willingly undertaken *in our behalf.* For others.

Rational it may be. Christian, I cannot believe. Suicide willfully disregards the suffering that we are called upon to undergo as a consequence of the very nature of our relationship to God Almighty. To abandon life *on our own terms* is truly to curve in upon ourselves. It is to refuse to drink the cup that Christ took for us, wants to share with us—and wants us to share with others.

Suicide is, to put it bluntly, selfishness carried to the ultimate extreme. It does not allow for any working of the power of redemptive suffering in the life of the individual, his or her friends, or his or her family. And, if there can be such a thing as rational suicide, it is by far the most selfish and the most arrogant for the very reason that it does not (cannot?) *rationally* consider the Christian teaching of redemptive suffering for others.

Chapter 9

What Does the Bible Say?

"Why is light given to him that is in misery,
    and life to the bitter in soul,
who long for death, but it comes not,
and who dig for it more than for his treasures;
who rejoice exceedingly,
    and are glad, when they find the grave?"
                —JOB 3:20–22

As is well known, the Book of Job is the one biblical book that deals with the question of suffering, both mental and physical, more consistently and at a deeper level than any other book. The writer is never weary of asking the question, Why?

True, Job did not commit suicide. But he is able to contemplate suicide in the context of his concern about the mystery of human suffering. "The bitter in soul who long for death" may not be a phrase that is found in the contemporary psychiatrist's lexicon, but hardly a day passes that a person who embodies just that phrase comes to the psychiatrist for help, and comes to pastors and priests for help. If the question Why? cannot be answered in some way that is satisfactory to that bitter soul, then suicide may well be the next step he or she takes.

Job did not commit suicide. Nor did the Apostle Paul. But he said:

> Christ will be honored in my body, whether by life or by death. For to me to live is Christ, and to die is gain. If it is to be life in the flesh, that means fruitful labor for me. Yet which I shall choose I cannot tell. I am hard-pressed between the two. My desire is to depart and be with Christ, for that is far better. But to remain in the flesh is more necessary on your account.
>
> —Philippians 1:20–24

There are two phrases in that passage that I should like to emphasize. "Yet which I shall choose I cannot tell" is the first. Clearly, Paul was not afraid to contemplate death—nor the idea that death could be chosen. True, Paul did not commit suicide. But neither Paul nor Job seems to have believed that his understanding of God constrained him from facing the thought of suicide.

Thus, to say, as some do today, that suicide is a crime against God does not seem to find support either from the greatest biblical wrestler with suffering or from the greatest biblical follower of Jesus Christ.

Even so, the phrase in Paul's letter that interests me most at this point is "to remain in the flesh is more necessary *on your account.*" I have emphasized "on your account" because it seems to me that this is the key to the whole of Jesus' teaching about both life and death. The suffering that Paul *knew* he would be called upon to endure so long as he remained alive was not for *himself.* Suicide was, indeed, a tempting "way out" of continued suffering. But he refused to choose it *because* of his conviction that his life and his service were intended to be for others—"on your account."

With this background, and I have only touched the surface of the implications of Job and Paul, let us look at the recorded instances of suicide in the Bible. To my knowledge, most of the recent books that deal with the biblical references to suicide are quite general in tone. These writers content themselves with a few statements to the effect that "there are six (or four) suicides reported in the Bible and there is no moral comment made about them." True, as far as it goes. But I believe that a great deal more can be said—and should be said.

I invite my reader to look up for himself or herself the following biblical references:

1. Judges 9:53   the story of Abimelech

2. Judges 16:29   the story of Samson

3. 2 Samuel 17:23   the story of Ahithophel

4. 1 Kings 16:18   the story of Zimri

5. 1 Chronicles 10:4–5 the story of Saul and his armor-bearer

6. Matthew 27:3   the story of Judas

Let us review these stories in succession. I believe that there is a common thread running through them that illustrates the point I am trying to make here.

1. Abimelech committed suicide because he could not bear the thought that his comrades would say of him "he was killed by a woman." Abimelech was thinking of himself.

2. Samson committed suicide because he wanted revenge against the Philistines for putting out one of his eyes. Samson was thinking of himself.

3. Ahithophel committed suicide "because his counsel was not followed." Ahithophel was thinking of himself.

4. Zimri's story is a bit ambiguous, but it looks as if he committed suicide because another man (Omri) was made king and/or because "the city had been taken"—which meant that he was discredited as a professional soldier. In either case, Zimri was thinking of himself.

5. Saul committed suicide because he could not bear the thought that his enemies would "make sport" of him when they captured him. Saul was thinking of himself. (So much so that he really caused the suicide of his armor-bearer?)

6. Judas committed suicide because he could not face the consequences of his betrayal of Jesus. Judas was thinking of himself.

Not one of these suicides even contemplated the idea that redemptive suffering *in behalf of others* might have solved his problem. To continue to live so as to redeem his actions, or lack of actions, through living and suffering for others would have been salvation instead of death.

There is a theory, an interpretation, about the death of Jesus with which I cannot agree. But it deserves to be considered for two reasons: It has come down to all from the earliest days of Christianity through the great Church Fathers, and it presents a stark contrast to the other suicides in the Bible.

The interpretation goes like this: Even non-Christians agree that Jesus of Nazareth was neither an ignorant fanatic nor a fool. All four Gospels depict a man who was fully in control of himself, who was well aware of the consequences of his words and actions. Thus, in the accounts of the events of the last week leading up to the Crucifixion, it appears that Jesus explicitly tried to prepare his disciples for his coming death. There can be no doubt that he knew what was at the end of the road for him.

If he knew that his actions would result in his death, why then did he not remain in Tyre and Sidon (Matt. 15:21 and Mark 7:24), or why did he not stay in Judea beyond the Jordan (Matt. 19:1)? Had he done so, it seems entirely likely that the Pharisees would have left him alone.

Was his death, then, a premeditated suicide? A rational suicide? Was it a deliberate sacrifice that, given his power and his understanding, he could easily have avoided? The Church Fathers Tertullian (A.D. 160–A.D. 230) and Origen (A.D. 185–A.D. 254) held that Jesus' death was a sacrificial suicide. John Donne, in the earliest essay in English on suicide, held the same view.

That is one interpretation. I cannot agree with it because I believe that Jesus acted out a divine drama that was not in any sense rational suicide.

In any case, the point I want to make here is that Jesus' death was certainly an intentional suffering *for others.* And I do not see that any of the other deaths by suicide recorded in the Bible were for the benefit of others.

The Christian Church, both Protestant and Roman Catholic, believing its teaching on suicide to be biblically based, has rested its case almost entirely upon the Commandment "Thou shalt not kill" (Ex. 20:13 and Deut. 5:17). It has long been recognized that this interpretation seems to rest on the teachings of Augustine and Aquinas. But there has always been the question, especially among Protestant theologians, Does "Thou shalt not kill" mean "Thou shalt not kill thyself"? And the secondary, but equally important question is, "Does to kill mean to murder?"

I think that a bit of biblical word study is useful here.

In Exodus 20:13 and Deuteronomy 5:17 the Hebrew word used is *ratsach.* Here, and at every other place in the Old Testament where it is used, *ratsach* means "to murder" or "a murderer" (see Deut. 4:42; 1 Kings 21:19; Hosea 4:2). But both the King James and the Revised Standard versions of the English Bible translate the word *ratsach* as "kill." Yet there are at least five other Hebrew words that mean "kill" and not "murder."

The same thing has happened in our translations of the New Testament word. In Matthew 5:21 and Mark 10:19 (KJV and RSV), when Jesus is recalling the words of the Commandments, the English says "kill," but the Greek is *phoneuo*—"to murder." (The New English Bible, and other contemporary translations such as The Good News For Modern Man, have made the correction. But the damage has been done long ago and is widespread. It will not be easily repaired.)

There is a difference in both English and the biblical language between the words "kill" and "murder." Murder means "the unlawful killing of a human being with malice aforethought." Synonyms are "assassination" and "homicide." Kill, on the other hand, means "to cause to die," to deprive of life, and (the ninth usage in my dictionary) "to commit murder." The dictionary goes on to say that "kill is the general word with no implication of the manner, agent, or cause of killing or the nature of what is killed."

Why, then, do our authorized English translations consistently use the general word "kill" when the Sixth Commandment specifically uses the word for "murder"? Why is the same thing repeated when the Hebrew word is correctly translated in Greek—but not in English?

There is no Hebrew word for "suicide." That word did not even occur in English until very recently. It means "the intentional taking of one's own life." It does *not* mean "to murder."

There are two or three theories in connection with Christian teaching as to why this change in the meaning of the two words has occurred. The one that is probably closest to the mark is found in Doris Portwood's book *Common-Sense Suicide: The Final Right.* (I cannot agree with the conclusions reached in her book, but her account is probably historically accurate.)

The early Christians brought a new attitude toward suicide by taking a fanatic delight in the prospect of instant salvation. There was no shortage of candidates for the tortures of the arena: a martyr's death meant a reserved seat among the blessed in heaven. These suicides were, in today's language (and *in the Roman Catholic legal view*) [italics mine], passive rather than active. The primitive Christians did not fall on the sword or hold the hemlock cup to their own lips, but they walked willingly—men, women and children— into situations (often deliberately provoked situations) that meant not only death but death of a most grim variety.

The mass suicide of early Christians, however, threatened to decimate the earthly population of the saved by removing them all to the promised afterlife. Reforms were needed, and came in the 4th to the 6th centuries A.D.

The Council of Braga in A.D. 563 specifically condemned suicide (codifying an attitude that had been emerging) and this condemnation was affirmed by later councils. The rationalization for the ban was a broadened interpretation of the commandment "Thou shalt not kill" to include self-destruction. St. Augustine developed the argument that because life is a gift of God, the rejection of life is a rejection of God and God's will—and thus a sin. Because suicide allowed no time for repentance it was extraordinarily sinful.

Although the Augustinian line of reasoning took much from Plato's *Phaedo* (man as a property of the gods) and nothing from the Bible, it persisted as the basic Christian doctrine. Suicide became and continues to be a sin; it was, under a State Church, equally a crime.[1]

Portwood's remark that Augustine had to go to Plato to find some justification for his doctrine, since he could find none in the Bible, deserves to be followed up by a closer look at the relevant biblical material.

I have already mentioned Paul's view of death for himself. But it should be stressed that those who are of the Christian faith too often refuse to believe what was one of Paul's strongest teachings: Death is not to be feared. "For since we believe that Jesus died and rose again, even so, through Jesus, God will bring with him those who have fallen asleep" (1 Thess. 4:14). "For God has not destined us for wrath, but to obtain salvation through our Lord Jesus Christ, who died for us so that whether we wake or sleep we might live with him" (1 Thess. 5:9–10). And perhaps Paul's most-quoted conviction: "O death, where is thy victory? O death, where is thy sting?" (1 Cor. 15:55).

It seems clear that our twentieth century fear of death, and our placing it into an almost unmentionable category, as if it were somehow unnatural, is peculiar to contemporary society. But it is not the norm, either in Christian or secular history, as any reading of history will demonstrate. (See Barbara Tuchman's excellent book *A Distant Mirror: The Calamitous Fourteenth Century*, Alfred A. Knopf, 1978.)

Probably, in both the secular and the religious world, the attitude expressed by the writer of Ecclesiastes is more characteristic of the feeling about death in earlier ages: "For everything there is a season, and a time for every matter under heaven: a time to be born, and a time to die" (Eccles. 3:2).

It is enlightening, therefore, in a discussion such as this, to look through the Bible not just for examples of suicides but also for attitudes toward death. There are more than one would expect, but here are a few of them:

When life appeared to be more than he cared to bear, Jonah "asked that he might die, and said, 'It is better for me to die than to live'" (Jon. 4:8).

When Jesus tried to prepare his followers for his own death, "Thomas, called the Twin, said to his fellow disciples, 'Let us also go, that we may die with him'" (John 11:16).

As we have seen Paul thought it a bit unusual for a man to volunteer to die, but not improbable: "While we were yet helpless, at the right time Christ died for the ungodly. Why, one will hardly die for a righteous man—though perhaps for a good man one will even dare to die" (Rom. 5:6–7).

When the writer of the Book of Revelation was describing his vision of the Apocalypse, he wrote: "And in those days men will seek death and will not find it; they will long to die, and death flies from them" (Rev. 9:6).

My point here is that death, whether self-inflicted or not, has throughout history been assumed as part and parcel of life. True, the biblical attitude is one of respect for life—but not *idolatry* of it. And there is a difference between the biblical attitude and the Roman indifference to life. But even here the biblical conception is a long way from what became the official Christian doctrine in later years (and remains so in our time).

Alvarez, perhaps, has an accurate historical summary of the situation that has come down to us:

> When the bishops decided that suicide was a crime, they were in some way emphasizing the moral distance traveled from pagan Rome, where suicide was habitual and even honored. Yet what began as moral tenderness and enlightenment finished as the legalized and sanctified atrocities by which the body of the suicide was degraded, his memory defamed, his family persecuted. So although the idea of suicide as a crime was a late, relatively sophisticated invention of Christianity, more or less foreign to the Judeo-Christian tradition, it spread like a fog across Europe because its strength came from primitive fears, prejudices and superstitions which had survived despite Christianity, Judaism and Hellenism. Given the barbarity of the Dark and Middle Ages, it was no doubt inevitable that the savage mind should once again have its way.[2]

And so we have a curious situation: Because religious law always precedes secular law (or at least has done so in Western society), we have supported the injunctions against suicide and the efforts at suicide prevention by secular law. "Thou shalt not kill" is the theological ground for that law. Yet, in the case of suicide, that precept does not appear to be based on a true interpretation of the Bible. Robert B. Reeves has a summary statement that may very well describe our present situation: "We have perverted the Judeo-Christian tradition into a belief that biological existence *per se* is of supreme value, and on the basis of that interpretation have been side-tracked into an ethical dilemma of ghastly proportions."[3]

The ethical dilemma that we face is before us because we have not understood, been unwilling to understand, what the Bible really says about death and suicide.

To sum up: In our day the problem of suicide is a tremendously complicated one. When we go to the Bible for guidance, it appears that what we find is an insistence that intentional death must be viewed as suffering—and not for oneself alone. It must include the kind of redemptive suffering enacted by the death of Jesus.

only I
did that.

Afterword

Since St. Augustine's time, the Christian tradition has held that suicide ignores the Law of God and all of the recognized rules of the life-giving forces. Suicide represents failure on a very mysterious level, a level that is hard to comprehend. Usually, it leaves family and friends stunned, confused, and shaken in their own faith.

It seems clear now that the time has come when the act of suicide will be embraced by more and more people as society in general accepts the cult of death. This is one of the reasons that I have presented the whole range of views about suicide in this book. But, in the end, my appeal to my readers and to the world is summed up in three words: "Don't do it!"

Notes

CHAPTER 1

1. *Monday Morning,* 31 March 1980, pp. 11–12.
2. Ibid., p. 12.
3. Doris Portwood, *Common-Sense Suicide: The Final Right.* (New York: Dodd, Mead & Co., 1978), p. 32.
4. Linnea Pearson and Ruth Bryant Purtilo, *Separate Paths: Why People End Their Lives.* (New York: Harper & Row, 1977), p. 136.
5. *New York Times,* 26 February 1975.
6. Dietrich Bonhoeffer, *Ethics.* (New York: Macmillan & Co., 1965), p. 166.
7. Pearson and Purtilo, *Separate Paths,* p. 67.
8. P. R. Baelz, "Suicide: Some Theological Reflections," in *Suicide: The Philosophical Issues,* eds. M. Pabst Battin and David J. Mayo (New York: St. Martin's Press, 1980), p. 82.

CHAPTER 2

1. Raymond A. Moody, Jr., *Life After Life* and *Reflections on Life After Life,* (Carmel, N.Y.: Guideposts; 1975), p. 174.
2. Ibid., p. 174.

3. Ibid., p. 175.
4. *The Tampa Tribune Times,* 27 July 1980, p. 9.
5. George G. Ritchie, *Return From Tomorrow* (Waco, Tex.: Chosen Books, 1978), p. 16.
6. George G. Ritchie, "I Found Life Beyond Death," *Fate,* December 1970, p. 11.
7. Ritchie, *Return From Tomorrow,* p. 56.
8. William Stainton Moses, *Spirit Teachings* (London: London Spiritualist Alliance, 1937), p. 17.
9. Allen Kardec, *The Spirits' Book* (Brasil: Ed tora LTD A), p. 378.
10. Ibid., p. 379.
11. Ibid., p. 381.
12. Ibid., p. 381.
13. Ibid., p. 382.
14. Alvin Boyd Kuhn, *Theosophy* (New York: Henry Holt and Co., 1930), p. 167.
15. Book of Common Prayer (1928), p. 54.
16. Annie Besant, *The Ancient Wisdom* (London: Theosophical Publishing Society, 1899), p. 115.
17. Ibid., p. 116.
18. *States After Death,* The Theosophy Co., p. 22.
19. Manly Palmer Hall, *Reincarnation: The Cycle of Necessity* (Los Angeles: Philosophical Research Society, 1978), p. 171.
20. Ibid., p. 171.
21. Philip T. Weller, *The Roman Ritual* (Milwaukee: Bruce Publishing Co., 1964), p. 519.
22. Ibid., p. 522.
23. Religious News Service Release, 18 February 1958.

CHAPTER 3

1. E. L. Abel, *Moon Madness* (New York: Fawcett, 1976), p. 140.
2. Ibid., p. 141.
3. Webb Garrison, *Strange Facts About Death* (Nashville: Abingdon, 1978), p. 99.
4. Book of Common Prayer (1928), p. 80.

5. William E. Hulme, *Am I Losing My Faith?* (Philadelphia: Fortress Press, 1971), p. 51.
6. Book of Common Prayer (1928), p. 332.
7. W. Cosby Bell, *If a Man Die* (New York: Charles Scribner's Son, 1934), p. 199.

CHAPTER 4

1. Religious News Service Release, 2 March 1962.
2. Religious News Service Release, 17 October 1969.
3. Religious News Service Release, 21 October 1975.
4. Elisabeth Kubler-Ross, *Questions and Answers on Death and Dying* (New York: Macmillan Publishing Co., 1974), p. 56.
5. Ibid., p. 58.

CHAPTER 5

1. Th. Haenel, F. Brunner, and R. Battegay, "Renal Dialysis and Suicide: Occurrence in Switzerland and in Europe," *Comparative Psychiatry* 21 (March/April 1980): p. 140.
2. "High Rate of Suicide Among M.D.'s on Probation Reported," *Physician's Management,* August 1980, p. 17.
3. Manly Palmer Hall, *Philosophical Research Journal* (Winter 1971): p. 67.
4. Edwin S. Shneidman, "Suicide—The Will to Die," National Association of Blue Shield Plans, (1973).
5. William V. Rauscher, *The Spiritual Frontier.* New York: Doubleday & Co., 1975. p. 6ff.

CHAPTER 6

1. Karl Menninger, *Man Against Himself.* (New York: Harcourt, Brace & World, 1966), p. 17.
2. *New York Times,* 21 September 1980.
3. Edwin S. Shneidman, ed., *Essays in Self-Destruction,* (New York: Jason Aronson, 1967), p. xv.

4. Louis Wekstein, *Handbook of Suicidology: Principles, Problems and Practices.* (New York: Brunner/Masel, 1979), p. 3.
5. Ibid., p. 8.
6. Calvin J. Frederick and Louise Lague, *Dealing With the Crisis of Suicide.* Public Affairs Pamphlet No. 406A. Ninth Printing, November 1979, Public Affairs Committee, p. 3.
7. Associated Press News Report, 12 May 1980.
8. Paul Friedman, "Suicide Among Police," in *Essays in Self-Destruction,* ed. Edwin S. Shneidman (New York: Jason Aronson, 1967), pp. 415.
9. Ibid., p. 417.

CHAPTER 7

1. A. Alvarez, *The Savage God: A Study of Suicide.* (New York: Bantam Books, 1972), p. 206.
2. James Hillman, *Suicide and the Soul.* (San Francisco: Harper & Row, 1964), p. 15.
3. John Florio, trans., *The Essayes of Michael Lord of Montaigne,* vol. II, (London: Oxford University Press, 1929), p. 25.
4. David Hume, *The Philosophical Works of David Hume,* vol. IV. (Boston: Little, Brown & Co., 1854), p. 362.
5. Josephus, *The Jewish War* 2. 18. 4.
6. *The New Catholic Encyclopedia,* Vol. 13. (New York: McGraw-Hill, Inc., 1968), p. 782.
7. Ibid., p. 783.
8. David Wilkerson, *Suicide: A Killer Is Stalking the Land.* (Old Tappan, N.J.: Fleming H. Revel, 1978), p. 30.
9. Ibid., p. 33f.
10. Ibid., p. 59.
11. Arthur Schopenhauer, *The World As Will and Idea,* vol. III. (London: Routledge and Kegan Paul,), p. 382.
12. Herbert A. Tonne, "Suicide: Is It Authoeuthanasia?" *The Humanist,* July/August 1979, p. 44.
13. Thomas Szasz, "The Myth of Radical Illness." *Newsweek,* October 29, 1973.

CHAPTER 8

1. Derek Humphry and Ann Wickett, *Jean's Way.* (London: Quartet Books, 1978), p. 29.
2. Seneca, *Epistulae Morales,* vol. II, trans. R. M. Gumere, Loeb Classical Library, (Cambridge, Mass.: Harvard University Press, 1931), p. 210.
3. A. Alvarez, *The Savage God: A Study of Suicide.* (New York: Bantam Books, 1972), p. 61.
4. Ibid., p. 62.

CHAPTER 9

1. Doris Portwood, *Common-Sense Suicide: The Final Right.* (New York: Dodd, Mead & Co., 1978), pp. 22–23.
2. A. Alvarez, *The Savage God: A Study of Suicide.* (New York: Bantam Books, 1972), p. 50.
3. Robert B. Reeves, Jr., in an address to The First Euthanasia Conference, November 23, 1968.

For Further Reading:
A Selected Bibliography

BOOKS

Alvarez, A. *The Savage God: A Study of Suicide.* New York: Bantam Books, 1970.

Augustine. *The City of God: Books I–VII.* Translated by D. B. Zema and G. G. Walsh. In *The Church Fathers: A New Translation,* vol. 8. New York: Deferrari, 1950.

Barth, Karl. *Church Dogmatics,* Vol. 3, *The Doctrine of Creation.* Translated by A. T. Mackay, T. H. L. Parker et. al. Edinburgh: T. & T. Clark, 1961.

Battin, M. Pabst, and David J. Mayo. *Suicide: The Philosophical Issues.* New York: St. Martin's Press, 1980.

Beck, Robert N., and John B. Orr. *Ethical Choice: A Case Study Approach.* New York: The Free Press, 1970.

Coleman, William L. *Understanding Suicide.* Elgin, Ill.: David C. Cook Publishing Co., 1979.

Danto, Bruce L., and A. H. Kutscher, eds. *Suicide and Bereavement.* New York: Arno Press, 1978.

Durkheim, Emile. *Suicide.* New York: The Free Press, 1951.

Ebon, Martin. *The Evidence for Life After Death.* New York: Signet Books, 1977.

———. *The Signet Handbook of Parapsychology.* New York: Signet Books, 1978.

121

Grollman, Earl R. *Suicide: Prevention, Intervention, Postvention.* Boston: Beacon Press, 1971.

Haim, Andre. *Adolescent Suicide.* Translated by A. M. Sheridan Smith. New York: International Universities Press, 1974.

Hatton, Corinne. *Suicide Assessment and Intervention.* New York: Appleton-Century-Crofts, 1976.

Hewett, John H. *After Suicide.* Philadelphia: Westminster Press, 1980.

Hillman, James. *Suicide and The Soul.* New York: Harper & Row, 1964.

Klagsbrun, Francine. *Too Young to Die.* Boston: Houghton Mifflin Co., 1976.

Kline, Nathan S. *From Sad To Glad.* New York: Ballantine Books, 1974.

Kubler-Ross, Elisabeth. *Questions and Answers on Death and Dying.* New York: Macmillan Publishing Co., 1974.

Langone, John. *Death Is a Noun: A View of the End of Life.* New York: Dell Publishing Co., 1972.

Lester, Gene, and David Lester. *Suicide: The Gamble With Death.* Englewood Cliffs N.J.: Prentice-Hall, 1971.

Lunde, Donald T., *Murder and Madness.* New York: W. W. Norton Publishing Co., 1975.

Madison, Arnold, *Suicide and Young People.* Seabury Press: New York, 1980

Maguire, D. C. *Death by Choice.* New York: Schocken Books, 1975.

Masaryk, Thomas G. *Suicide and the Meaning of Civilization.* Chicago: The University of Chicago Press, 1970.

Menninger, Karl. *Man Against Himself.* New York: Harcourt, Brace & World, 1938.

Moody, Raymond A., Jr. *Life After Life.* New York: Bantam Books, 1975.

———. *Life After Life* and *Reflections on Life After Life.* Carmel, N.Y.: Guideposts, 1975.

Mundy, Jon. *Learning To Die.* Evanston, Ill.: Spiritual Frontiers Fellowship, 1973.

Pearce-Higgins, J. D., and G. Stanley Whitby, eds. *Life, Death and Psychical Research.* London: Rider and Co., 1973.

Perlin, Seymour, ed. *A Handbook for the Study of Suicide.*

New York: Oxford University Press, 1975.

Plato. *Phaedo.* Translated by Benjamin Jowett. In *The Dialogues of Plato,* 2 Vols. New York: Random House, 1937.

Portwood, Doris. *Common-Sense Suicide: The Final Right.* New York: Dodd, Mead & Co., 1978.

Reynolds, David K., and Norman L. Farberow. *Suicide Inside and Out.* Berkeley: University of California Press: 1976.

Ring, Kenneth, *Life at Death.*—A Scientific investigation of the near-death experience. Coward, McCann & Geoghegan: New York, 1980

Ritchie, George G. *Return From Tomorrow.* Waco, Tex.: Chosen Books, 1978.

Russell, O. Ruth. *Freedom to Die.* New York: Human Sciences Press, 1975.

Shneidman, Edwin S., ed. *Essays in Self-Destruction.* New York: Science House, 1967.

Shneidman, Edwin S., and Norman L. Farberow. *The Psychology of Suicide.* New York: Science House, 1970.

Shneidman, Edwin, *Voices of Death.* New York: Harper & Row, 1980.

Stengel, Erwin. *Suicide and Attempted Suicide.* Baltimore: Penguin Books, 1964.

Tweedale, Charles L. *Man's Survival After Death.* London: Richards, 1931.

West, Jessamyn. *The Woman Said Yes: Encounters With Life and Death.* New York: Harcourt Brace Jovanovich, 1976.

Wilkerson, David. *Suicide: A Killer Is Stalking The Land!* Old Tappan, N.Y.: Fleming H. Revell, 1978.

ARTICLES AND ESSAYS

Bemporad, Jules. "Psychodynamics of Depression and Suicide in Children and Adolescents." In *Severe and Mild Depression and the Psychotherapeutic Approach,* by Silvano Avieti, and Jules Bemporad. New York: Basic Books, 1978.

Brandt, R. B. "The Morality and Rationality of Suicide." In *A Handbook For The Study of Suicide,* edited by Seymour Perlin. New York: Oxford University Press, 1975.

Calhoun, James F. "Suicide." In *Abnormal Psychology,* by

James F. Calhoun and John Ross Acocella. New York: Random House, 1977.

Farberow, Norman L. "The Cultural History of Suicide." In *Suicide in Different Cultures,* edited by Norman L. Farberow. Baltimore: University Park Press, 1975.

Hall, Manly P. *Reincarnation: The Cycle of Necessity.* Los Angeles: The Philosophical Research Society, 1978.

Hendin, Herbert. "A Saner Policy On Suicide." *Psychology Today,* May 1979, pp. 115–116.

Holland, R. F. "Suicide." In *Moral Problems: A Collection of Philosophical Essays,* edited by James Rachels. New York: Harper & Row, 1971.

Hume, David. "On Suicide." In *The Philosophical Works of David Hume,* vol. 4. Boston: Little, Brown & Co., 1854.

Portwood, Doris. "A Right To Suicide?" *Psychology Today,* January 1978, pp. 66–76.

Pretzel, Paul. "Philosophical and Ethical Considerations of Suicide Prevention." *Bulletin of Suicidology,* July 1968, pp. 30–38.

Silving, Helen. "Suicide and Law." In *Clues To Suicide,* edited by Edwin S. Shneidman and Norman L. Farberow. New York: McGraw-Hill, 1957.

Steppacher, Robert C., and Judith S. Mausner. "Suicide in Male and Female Physicians." *Journal of the American Medical Association* 228:323–328.

Stevenson, Ian, *Twenty Cases Suggestive of Reincarnation.* New York: American Society for Psychical Research, 1966.

Szasz, Thomas. "The Ethics of Suicide." *Antioch Review* 31:1–17.

Tonne, Herbert A. "Suicide: Is It Authoeuthanasia?" *The Humanist,* July/August 1979, pp. 45–46.

PAMPHLETS

Allen, Nancy H., and Michael L. Peck. *Suicide In Young People.* The American Association of Suicidology.

Farberow, Norman L. *Suicide.* University Programs Modular Studies. Morristown, N.J.: General Learning Corporation, 1974.

Fawcett, Jan. *Before It's Too Late.* The American Association of Suicidology.

Frederick, Calvin J., and Louise Lague. *Dealing With The Crisis of Suicide.* The Public Affairs Committee, Pamphlet No. 406A. 1972.

Freese, Arthur S. *Adolescent Suicide: Mental Health Challenge.* The Public Affairs Committee, Pamphlet No. 569. 1979.

Lee, A. Russell. *Suicide in Youth and What You Can Do About It.* The Suicide Prevention and Crisis Center of San Mateo County, California, in cooperation with The American Association of Suicidology.

Ogg, Elizabeth. *Help for Emotional and Mental Problems.* The Public Affairs Committee, Pamphlet No. 567. 1979.

Shneidman, Edwin S., and Philip Mandelkorn. *Suicide—It Doesn't Have To Happen.* The American Association of Suicidology.

Teicher, Joseph D. *Why Adolescents Kill Themselves.* Mental Health Reports, No. 4. United States Department of Health, Education and Welfare. Publication No. 5026. January 1970.

ENCYCLOPEDIA AND DICTIONARY ARTICLES

Douglas, Jack D., Edwin S. Shneidman, and Norman L. Farberow. "Suicide," *The International Encyclopedia of Social Science,* Vol. 15, pp. 375–396. New York: Macmillan and Co., 1968.

Friedman, Paul. "Suicide," *The Encyclopedia of Mental Health,* pp. 1890–1983.

Kane, T. C. "Suicide," *The New Catholic Encyclopedia,* Vol. 13, pp. 781–783. New York: McGraw-Hill Co., 1968.

Revel, Hirschel. "Suicide," *The Universal Jewish Encyclopedia,* pp. 93–94. New York: KTAV Publishing Co., 1969.

Shneidman, Edwin S. "Suicide," *Encyclopedia Britannica,* Vol. 21, pp. 384a,b,c,d–385. 1978.

Smith, David H., and Seymour Perlin. "Suicide," *The Encyclopedia of Bioethics,* pp. 1618–1626.

Vander Heeren, A. "Suicide," *The Catholic Encyclopedia,* Vol. XIV, pp. 326–328. New York: The Encyclopedia Press, 1912.

Young, E. W. "Suicide," *The Interpreters' Dictionary of the Bible,* Vol. 4, pp. 453–454. New York: Abingdon Press, 1962.

TAPE CASSETTES, REPRINTS, AND BIBLIOGRAPHIES

The following material may be obtained from The Center for Information on Suicide, Suite 53, 6867 Golfcrest Drive, San Diego, California 92119. The code following the entry is the order number of the item.

CASSETTES

"A Suicide Note" (Speaker unknown—a young drug addict suicide.) (T-1)

"Do Suicide Prevention Centers Prevent Suicides?" James Selkin. (T-2)

"The Chronically Suicidal Person." Mary Savage. (T-3)

"Suicide Among the Elderly." Marvin Miller. (T-4)

"Suicides in Institutional Settings." David Reynolds. (T-5)

"Physician Suicides." Jerry Bergman. (T-6)

"Golden Gate Bridge Suicides." Richard Seiden. (T-7)

"Suicide Among American Indians." James Shore. (T-8)

"The Nurse's Role in Suicide Prevention and Intervention." Corrine Hatton. (T-9)

"The Suicidogenic Family." Joseph Richman. (T-10)

"Suicide Intervention by Police and Paramedics." Bruce Danto. (T-11)

"The Relationship of Suicide and Homicide." David Lester. (T-12)

"The Ethics of Suicide Prevention." Paul Pretzel. (T-13)

"Suicide Among Women." Karin Wandrei. (T-14)

"Grief Support Groups for Survivors of Suicides." Elnora Ross. (T-15)

ARTICLES

"Surviving the Loss of a Loved One: An Inside Look at Grief Counseling." (A-1)

"Everything You've Always Wanted to Know About Suicide." (A-3)

"Suicide After Sixty." (A-4)

"What Suicide Notes Really Tell Us." (A-5)
"The Cooperation of Some Wives in Their Husbands' Suicides." (A-7)
"Protecting Your Family and Friends From Suicide." (A-8)
"How Can We Help the Suicidal Physician?" (A-11)
"The Geography of Suicide." (A-15)

BIBLIOGRAPHIES
"Suicide Among Blacks." (R-2)
"Suicide Among Physicians." (R-3)
"Suicide Among Women." (R-4)
"Suicide Among Children." (R-5)
"Suicide Among Adolescents." (R-6)
"Suicide Among College Students." (R-7)
"Suicide Among the Elderly." (R-8)
"Suicide Notes." (R-9)
"Suicide and Alcoholism." (R-11)
"Suicide Prevention and Intervention by Nurses." (R-12)
"Psychological Autopsies." (R-13)
"Books About Suicide." (R-14)
"The Influence of Parental Absence or Parental Suicide." (R-15)
"Suicides Among Homosexuals." (R-17)
"Suicides in the Military Services." (R-18)
"The Ethics of Suicide Prevention and Intervention." (R-19)
"Distinctions Between Attempted and Completed Suicides." (R-20)
"Autocides" (suicides disguised as auto accidents). (R-21)
"Legal Aspects of Suicide." (R-22)
"Suicide and the Police." (R-24)
"The Role of the Clergy in Suicide Prevention." (R-25)
"Suicide and Religion." (R-26)
"Survivors of Suicides." (R-28)
"Suicide and Drug Abuse." (R-29)
"1980 Master Bibliography on Suicidology." (R-30)